England

England

Revised Edition

BY JEAN F. BLASHFIELD

Enchantment of the World
Second Series

Children's Press®

A Division of Scholastic Inc.

NEW YORK   TORONTO   LONDON   AUCKLAND   SYDNEY
MEXICO CITY   NEW DELHI   HONG KONG
DANBURY, CONNECTICUT

Frontispiece: Beech trees in Hertfordshire, England

Consultant: Timothy J. Rickard, Professor of Geography, Central Connecticut State University, New Britain, Connecticut

Please note: All statistics are as up-to-date as possible at the time of publication.

Book production by Herman Adler

Library of Congress Cataloging-in-Publication Data

Blashfield, Jean F.
  England, revised edition / by Jean F. Blashfield—Rev. ed.
    p. cm. — (Enchantment of the world. Second series)
  Includes index.
  ISBN-10: 0-516-24869-3
  ISBN-13: 978-0-516-24869-1
  1. England—Juvenile literature. I. Title. II. Series.
  DA27.5.B58 2007
  942—dc22   2005028213

England

Cover photo:
Yorkshire Dales
National Park

Contents

Winchester College

A London police officer

This Precious Stone

IN 1993, ARCHAEOLOGISTS WERE DIGGING AT A SITE NEAR the town of Boxgrove in southern England. They were looking for clues about how early people in the region lived. One of the scientists noticed something unusual among the rocks. It was a bone. The archaeologists carefully dug the bone out from its rocky surroundings and found that it was a human shinbone. They later found teeth and stone tools at the same site. The person to whom these items belonged became known as Boxgrove Man.

Opposite: **Few trees grow on the quiet moorlands of southwestern England.**

The bones of Boxgrove Man are among the oldest human remains found in Europe.

Boxgrove Man was tall—6 feet (1.8 meters). He was a hunter-gatherer and a tool user. He lived at least five hundred thousand years ago. The bones of Boxgrove Man are the oldest human remains ever found in England. They are also among the oldest found in Europe.

At the time when Boxgrove Man lived, the island of Great Britain on which England sits was still connected to the rest of Europe. This was true for hundreds of thousands of years. But then, about eight thousand years ago, Great Britain began separating from the continent. Ocean filled the low-lying area between them. This new island would eventually be home to one of the most powerful nations on earth.

The remains found near Boxgrove have helped archaeologists understand how early people lived in England.

ENGLAND

- Cities of over 200,000 people
- Other cities
- ✪ Capital

0 _____ 80 miles

0 _____ 80 kilometers

England

Edinburgh

Scotland

Tweed R.

**UNITED
KINGDOM**

*Northumberland
National Park*

**Northern
Ireland**

Carlisle · Newcastle
upon Tyne · South Shields
· Sunderland
· Hartlepool
Stockton-on-Tees · Middlesborough
Darlington

Belfast

Whitehaven · *Lake District
National
Park* · *Yorkshire Dales
National
Park* · *North York Moors
National Park* · Scarborough

*Isle of
Man*

Barrow-in-
Furness · Lancaster · Bridlington

York · *Humber R.* · Kingston upon Hull

Irish Sea

Bradford · Leeds

Blackpool · Preston

Manchester · Sheffield · Grimsby

IRELAND

Liverpool · Lincoln · *The
Wash*

*North
Sea*

Chester · Crewe · *Peak District
National Park*

Stoke-on-Trent · Derby · Nottingham · *The Broads
National Park*

Stafford · *Trent R.* · Leicester · Peterborough · Norwich · Great
Yarmouth

Wolverhampton · Birmingham · Coventry · Ely · *R.* · Lowestoft

*Cardigan
Bay*

Wales

Worcester · Warwick · Rugby · *Ouse* · Cambridge · Ipswich

*Severn
R.* · Stratford-
upon-Avon · Bedford · Colchester

Great · Luton · Chelmsford

Gloucester · St. Albans · Southend-on-Sea

St. George's Channel

R. Thames · London

Cardiff · Swindon · Reading · Chatham · Margate

Bristol Channel · Bristol · Bath · Basingstoke · Windsor · Canterbury · Dover

Stonehenge · Guildford

*Exmoor
National Park* · *South Downs National Park* · Folkestone

Bideford · Wellington · *New Forest
National Park* · Boxgrove · Brighton · Hastings

*Celtic
Sea*

Southampton · Portsmouth · Eastbourne

Exeter · Poole · *The Solent* · Ventnor

*Dartmoor
National Park* · *Lyme Bay* · Bournemouth · *Isle
of Wight*

Plymouth · Torquay

*Isles of
Scilly* · Penzance · Dartmouth

St. Mary's · Falmouth

English Channel

Alderney

Guernsey · Sark

FRANCE

Jersey

N *S* *E* *W*

The ancient people who built Stonehenge brought the stones to the site from a quarry about 25 miles (40 km) away. Some of these huge stones weighed 25 tons.

Leaving a Mark

About five thousand years ago, people living in what is now England began to build one of the world's most amazing structures. It is called Stonehenge. It consists of immense rings of giant stones sunk into the earth. Even today, scholars don't know the exact purpose of these stones. It was likely related to religion. Stonehenge might have been an observatory that helped people understand the movement of the puzzling lights we call the stars, planets, sun, and moon. Every June 21, the longest day of the year, the sun rises exactly over a smaller stone set outside the circles. These days, hundreds of thousands of people make the journey to Stonehenge every year to see one of the marvels of human history.

Stonehenge is just one of many marvels found in England. This small country was the center of one of the mightiest nations on earth, a nation that ruled an empire that spanned the globe. Its political system has been copied by countries around the world. Its language has become one of the most widely spoken on earth. Its industry became the envy of the world. Its thinkers revolutionized science. Its literature is required reading for people everywhere. With its fabled history and proud traditions, its vibrant cities and quiet villages, England lies close to the heart of many people. In *Richard II*, by the famous playwright William Shakespeare, one character calls England, "This precious stone set in the silver sea . . . This blessed plot, this earth, this realm, this England."

Untangling Terms

What is England? And what is Britain? Great Britain? The British Isles? The United Kingdom? These names are often used interchangeably, but they actually mean different things.

The British Isles are a group of islands that include the big island of Great Britain, the smaller island of Ireland, and still smaller islands strewn around the coasts. England occupies about 54 percent of the island of Great Britain. It shares the island with Wales and Scotland.

The United Kingdom is a modern nation consisting of the once-separate nations of England, Wales, and Scotland. The United Kingdom also includes part of Ireland called Northern Ireland. The United Kingdom is often referred to as the UK.

The term *Britain* is short for Great Britain or the United Kingdom. A Briton is someone living on the island, especially in prehistory. Unlike the term *British*, *English* cannot be used for all the residents of the British Isles. The people from the northern part of Great Britain—Scotland—are Scots. Those from the western bulge of the island—Wales—are Welsh. Even the people who lived in England long ago weren't called English. The term is generally used only for the people who lived on the island after the Roman Empire abandoned it in about A.D. 400. That was when the tribes of Angles, Saxons, and Jutes invaded England from northern Europe and mingled. Together, these people came to be called by the single name *Anglish*. The name *England*, then, came from "Angle-land."

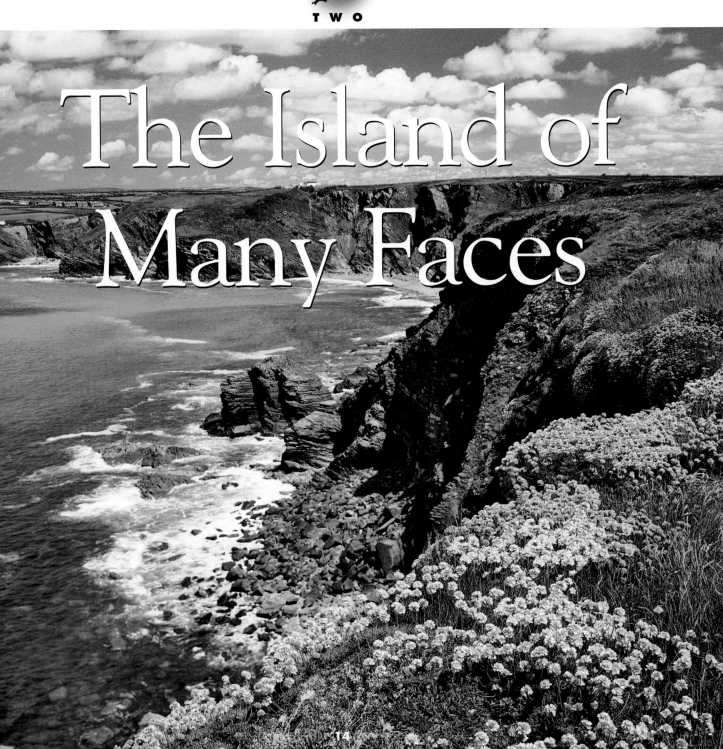

The Island of Many Faces

ENGLAND IS A NATION DOMINATED BY THE SEA. NO PLACE in the country is more than 75 miles (121 kilometers) from the ocean. Though England is small, only a little larger than the state of Louisiana, it has many different kinds of scenery. It has mountains, valleys, marshland, moors, big lakes, plains, and cliffs.

England is divided into forty counties. County names often end is *shire*, such as Berkshire. The counties are distributed among nine regions: South East, South West, London, East of England, East Midlands, West Midlands, Yorkshire and the Humber, North East, and North West.

Opposite: **Cornwall in western England is famous for its rugged cliffs.**

Stone walls and barns grace the scenic fields of Yorkshire Dales.

The Reappearing County

Rutland County, England's smallest county, is located in the East Midlands. It is so tiny that ten Rutland Counties could fit into the state of Rhode Island. In the 1970s, the government organized the county out of existence.

Rutland County did not exist for twenty-three years. During this time, the Rutlanders urged Parliament to bring Rutland County back. In 1997, they succeeded, and little Rutland County reappeared on maps.

A rocky stream winds through the Cheviot Hills along the border between England and Scotland.

England shares the island of Great Britain with Scotland and Wales. England's border with Scotland lies along the River Tweed and the Cheviot Hills, and then meanders southwest to the Solway Firth. (A firth is an arm of the sea that extends inland, often between cliffs.) The border with Wales runs southward in a wavy line from the mouth of the River Dee to the mouth of the Wye River on the Severn Estuary.

The remainder of England's border is its coastline on the North Sea, the Irish Sea, and the English Channel. Across the English Channel is France and the rest of Europe. At the Strait of Dover, England is just 22 miles (35 km) from France.

England's Geographic Features

Area: 50,352 square miles (130,410 sq km)

Highest elevation: Scafell Pike, 3,210 feet (978 m)

Lowest elevation: Usually sea level, but when the tide is out near Ely in the Fen Country, a small section of exposed land is actually several feet below sea level

Longest river: The Thames, 215 miles (346 km) long (in England)

Largest lake: Windermere, 10 miles (16 km) long

Average annual rainfall: East coast, 20 inches (50 cm); Western and northern hills, 40 inches (100 cm); Lake District, 130 inches (330 cm)

Largest city: Greater London

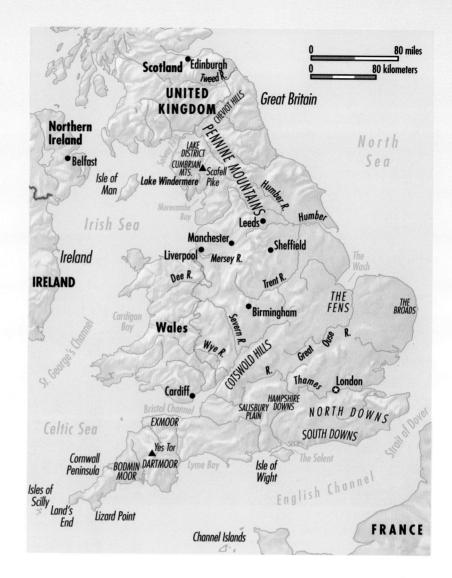

The Shape of the Land

The island of Great Britain is divided into highland and lowland regions. The highlands are mostly in Scotland, but they extend into England in the Pennine Mountains, often called the spine or the backbone of England. The Pennines curve down into central England, ending just southeast of

Windermere has been popular with tourists since 1847, when a railroad was built connecting it with points south.

Manchester. To the west of the Pennines is the Lake District. In this area, sixteen lakes lie amid steep mountainsides. Lake Windermere, at more than 10 miles (16 km) long, is the largest lake in England. Many people consider the Lake District the most beautiful part of England.

South of the Pennines is the region called the Midlands. This lowlands region was once the center of British industry. It is heavily populated, containing big cities such as Birmingham.

To the east of the Midlands lies a large, almost rectangular bay called the Wash. It is bordered by the Fens, which are grassy wetlands. Fens, like bogs, are spongy to walk on because they are made of ancient vegetation that has piled up and holds water. The fens were drained during the 1600s, creating almost 500,000 acres (200,000 hectares) of farmland. South of the Wash is a bulge of low, flat land called East Anglia.

Rivers and lakes crisscross the part of East Anglia called the Broads. This region is Great Britain's largest protected wetland.

The southwestern part of England is a peninsula known as the West Country. Lizard Point, near the tip of the peninsula, is the southernmost point of the English mainland. The westernmost point in England is Land's End, a short distance along the coast from Lizard Point. Land's End lies 3,290 miles (5,295 km) straight across uninterrupted ocean from North America. The West Country has several large moors—bleak, treeless areas. Low-growing evergreen plants called heather grow on the moors.

The Longships Lighthouse sits atop a rock just off the coast of Land's End. A lighthouse on the spot has warned ships of the dangerous coast since 1795.

London, the capital city, is in southeastern England. South of that are low, grassy, treeless chalk hills called the downs. Chalk is a type of soft limestone. In Uffington, west of London, there is a low hill on which ancient people carved the figure of a giant horse 374 feet (114 m) long. No one knows for sure when the horse was carved through the topsoil into the chalk beneath.

At the island's southeastern tip, the chalk is exposed. These are the famous "white cliffs of Dover." Parts of the soft chalk cliffs sometimes break off and fall into the sea.

The Uffington Horse is one of several large horses carved into England's chalk downs.

The major indentations in the coast of England are the estuaries of large rivers. Estuaries are the mouths of rivers, where freshwater and salt water mix. Estuaries are often home to abundant wildlife, and they often make good harbors for boats. The Humber River estuary, on the northeast coast, is one of the nation's largest. The Humber River served as a highway into the heart of England for Viking invaders.

The muddy waters of the Humber Estuary provide a home for millions of creatures, including seventy-six different species of fish.

The river Thames (TEHMZ) flows eastward across southern England. For hundreds of years, the Thames was the main highway to London. From 1450 to 1850, England had colder than normal weather. During this "Little Ice Age," the Thames often froze in winter, and Frost Fairs were held on the ice. The last fair was held in 1814. After that, the river was made deeper so that the tide could flow farther upriver, and the Thames no longer froze.

Keeping Central London Dry

Central London lies at sea level. When an unusually high tide, called a surge, moves up the river, the resulting flood can kill people and destroy buildings. The Thames Flood Barrier, which opened in 1984, prevents Central London from being flooded by such surges. The barrier consists of ten movable gates that line up across the river. Some of the gates sink into the riverbed when not in use so that river traffic can move.

When a surge threatens, the gates are raised and turned to form a steel wall. Each gate is more than 65 feet (20 m) high and weighs about 4,000 tons (3,600 metric tons).

Bristol Channel lies between the West Country and Wales. This huge bay leads to the estuary of the Severn River. Just north of the Welsh border on the River Dee is the estuary of the Mersey River. Liverpool, England's third-largest city, lies along the Mersey. The big industrial city of Manchester is connected to the Mersey by the Manchester Ship Canal.

Marking Time

At Greenwich on the river Thames, the Royal Observatory was built in 1675. An imaginary line runs through the Royal Observatory. It marks the 0° line of longitude, or prime meridian, which circles the Earth from the North Pole to the South Pole. All distances east and west around the world are measured from this line. Since the late 1800s, the prime meridian in Greenwich has also been used to keep track of time. Time zones are measured from Greenwich. And each new day comes first to Greenwich.

England Offshore

The Channel Islands are located in the English Channel, much closer to France than to England. Though they recognize Queen Elizabeth II as their monarch, they are, in fact, self-governing. So, too, is the Isle of Man, located in the Irish Sea. These islands have their own legislatures and laws, but the United Kingdom takes care of their international relations and defense.

Other islands near Great Britain are part of England. The Isle of Wight is off the southern coast. Ships coming into port at Southampton have to go around the island. The Isles of Scilly consist of more than a hundred small islands plus many rocks. They lie 25 to 36 miles (40 to 58 km) off the coast of Land's End. Only five of the islands are inhabited year-round. The largest is St. Mary's, where most of the people live.

"Looks Like Rain"

England is on the same latitude as Newfoundland, Canada. But while Newfoundland faces frigid winters, England's are milder. This is because of the Gulf Stream, a big ocean current that carries warm water from the Caribbean Sea to the British coast. The Gulf Stream lets flowers bloom in February and palm trees grow in southwestern England. The rain and warmth from the Gulf Stream keep England green throughout the year.

England's coastal areas are the warmest, with an average winter temperature of about 40°F (4°C). Hilly areas are much colder, especially in northern England. Only the South East is likely to average much above 60°F (16°C) in July and August. Anything above 75°F (24°C) is considered a heat wave. On August 20, 2003, the temperature at Gravesend reached 100°F (38°C), the highest temperature ever recorded in Britain.

Though England is famous for its rain, it does not actually add up to much. The constant winds coming across the ocean bring rain to England fairly evenly throughout the year, so that an average month may get a little rain on about half the days. But the total amount of rain over the course of the year is minimal. The Lake District averages 130 inches

England is famed for its cool, damp weather. Clouds often swoop in quickly, turning blue skies gray.

(330 centimeters) of rain each year, but can get up to 200 inches (500 cm). London gets only 20 inches (50 cm)—about the same as South Dakota. Snow falls in the London area only four or five times each winter and rarely stays on the ground for long.

Devastating Weather

Hurricanes form in the Caribbean, brush past the United States, and then turn seaward into the Atlantic, but they rarely survive long enough to hit Europe. Great Britain has had major windstorms, however. On the night of October 15–16, 1987, winds blowing 100 miles per hour (160 kph) hit southern England. These were the highest winds ever recorded in London. They uprooted millions of trees, including at least five hundred rare, old trees at Kew Gardens. Twenty-seven months later, another storm hit the British Isles and Europe with winds as high as 110 mph (177 kph). Forty-six people died in Britain, and nearly as many deaths were reported on the European continent.

London was once famous for its terrible fogs. They were called pea-soup fogs because they were thick and greenish. They were so thick that people could not see more than a few feet away. Some people also called them killer fogs because they could be deadly for people with lung problems. It wasn't the fog itself that caused the health problems; it was pollution in the air from the burning coal used for heat and industry. After burning coal in cities was outlawed in 1956, killer fogs disappeared.

Looking at English Cities

Birmingham (right), which lies in the West Midlands, is England's second-largest city after London. It is one of England's largest industrial centers. Birmingham produces a lot of steel and has many highly skilled engineers, making it an ideal spot for the British auto industry. Long before the auto industry arrived, Birmingham was famous for its military equipment, jewelry, and other crafts.

Liverpool (left), located on the Mersey River, boasts one of the largest harbors in the world and is a center of shipping and manufacturing. Liverpool is perhaps most famous for having produced the Beatles, the pop music group that dominated the charts in the 1960s. Today, its industry is in decline, and many of its port facilities have been converted to stores and apartments.

Sheffield, England's fourth-largest city, is located on the Don River in the north-central part of the country. Sheffield has been famous for its knives and other cutting tools since the Middle Ages. In *The Canterbury Tales*, a collection of stories written in the late 1300s, Geoffrey Chaucer referred to a "Sheffield thwitel," the ancestor of the modern pocketknife.

Natural England

ENGLAND IS A CROWDED COUNTRY. FORTUNATELY, NATURE has always been important to the people who live there. For centuries, cities have had parks. Well before the environmental movement caught on around the world, England made an effort to create greenbelts, areas around major cities where people could not build.

Pathways across private land are traditionally kept open. These public rights-of-way allow the English, who are great walkers, to explore areas of the country that they might not otherwise see. England has 140,000 miles (225,000 km) of

Opposite: **The West Dart River tumbles through Dartmoor National Park in western England.**

Walkers make their way down the Ridgeway National Trail, north of London. This ancient track is England's oldest road.

public paths. There are fifteen footpaths called National Trails that take hikers through particularly scenic areas. For example, the Pennine Way extends the length of the Pennines, about 270 miles (435 km). While out walking, people may spot wildflowers such as bluebells, snowdrops, primroses, and poppies. Heathers and whortleberries grow on the moors.

Only about 9 percent of English land is forested. This is less than Great Britain as a whole and far less than the rest of Europe. This percentage has actually risen in recent years because owners of agricultural land are encouraged to return land to forest in exchange for a small annual payment. This plan increases the amount of forest, which serves both as wildlife habitat and as a source of timber that doesn't have to be imported.

Wildflowers bring color to the forests in the spring.

Gardens of England

Many of England's wild areas have given way to agriculture and housing, but the English have made up for it by enthusiastically planting gardens. Certain parts of England have been planted for so long that it's hard to tell what is natural. More than five thousand varieties of plants from all over the world grow in the Abbey Garden on Tresco, one of the Isles of Scilly. The garden was started almost a thousand years ago.

The Royal Botanic Gardens at Kew, near London, was founded in 1759. Its goal is to collect as many types of plants as possible from around the world. The Seed Bank at Kew holds the seeds of some thirteen thousand species of plants. It is hoped that if scientists someday discover that a certain species no longer found in the wild is useful in medicine, Kew will have the seeds.

The Royal Botanic Gardens at Kew is one of London's most popular sites. More than a million people visit it every year.

Hedgerows line many of the narrow roads in the English countryside.

Most of natural England has been turned into farm fields or pasture. But many fields have long been enclosed by rows of bushes that have grown old and tangled. Called hedgerows, they are natural homes for many birds and small mammals. Unfortunately, old hedgerows are now being cut down in order to enlarge fields for modern machinery.

Wild Creatures

Gone are the wolves and the wild boars—they were hunted out of existence long ago. But England still has many large mammals.

Exmoor National Park and the Lake District have red deer, while the roe deer is found only in the West Country. The fallow deer is found in many areas of England. The European hedgehog can be found everywhere, even in the bushes of busy London. This little mammal, often compared to the porcupine, looks and feels like a large pinecone. Some species of hares are native to England, but the country had no rabbits until they were brought in by the Romans nearly two thousand years ago. The rabbits took over large parts of the

Roe deer were virtually wiped out in England in the 1700s. They were reintroduced to England in the 1800s.

countryside, often feeding on gardens. Badgers are also common on agricultural land. The red fox is found throughout England, even in the suburbs. Otters are common along the riverbanks, and several species of seals are found along the western coasts.

The English have long been avid bird-watchers. Many people maintain lifetime lists of birds they have seen and identified. The variety of habitats found in England provides homes for many species of birds. Robins, thrushes, skylarks, and magpies live in English gardens. Swans and ducks grace the lakes, while curlews, cormorants, and terns make their homes at the seaside. Many other birds, such as swallows from Africa and cranes from Europe, pass over England on their way north or south. The roseate tern and skylark are among the birds that are now endangered.

Red foxes will eat almost anything. Many now live close to cities and towns because they like the variety of plants they can find there.

Hoofbeats on the Moors

England's eerie moors are home to some surprising hoofed animals—wild ponies. Actually, they're not quite wild: Naturalists watch over them to make sure they are healthy, and the creatures are used to being approached by people. Once a year, the ponies are herded together, checked, and counted. If there are too many animals for the area, some young animals are sold to private citizens.

Lake District National Park

The Lake District lies in northwest England, just south of Scotland. Most of the Lake District is protected in Lake District National Park, the country's largest national park. The park is a jumble of sparkling lakes, low craggy mountains, and pretty stone villages. Many visitors enjoy the steep walking trails over the hills, which offer spectacular views.

Fourteen million people visit the Lake District each year, making it the second most visited place in England, after London. In recent years, the Lake District has become as famous for its traffic jams as for its beauty. But for many, the quiet magical corners they can find tucked away make the Lake District worth the headaches.

England has nine national parks. Unlike national parks in most other countries, the land in England's national parks is generally privately owned. The Parks Authority works with the owners to manage the land carefully and plan which paths and areas can be open to the public.

Dartmoor is England's oldest national park. It was declared a national park in 1951. Dartmoor is famed for its tors, large hills with huge granite stones on top. Yes Tor, which rises to more than 2,000 feet (600 m), is Dartmoor's tallest tor. Exmoor, nearby, is gentler, with some spectacular scenery on the Bristol Channel. The Broads, an area of wetlands and streams in Norfolk and Suffolk, became a national park in 1989.

Much of Dartmoor National Park is covered by grass or moorland. Visitors come to the park to enjoy the peaceful isolation.

Making History

THE EARLY HUMANS WHO ENTERED THE LAND NOW CALLED England were hunters. They may have been hunting rhinoceroses, lions, and cave bears. They probably didn't stay on the island long. Then, about five thousand years ago, other humans crossed the English Channel from France to England. They were farmers who took advantage of England's climate. They buried their dead in huge burial mounds. They also began to build monumental stone circles.

Opposite: **Guildford Castle was built nearly a thousand years ago. Almost all that remains is a tower.**

England's earliest people buried their dead in large mounds. Some of these are still visible today.

About the time the oldest part of Stonehenge was built, the Beaker people, known only from their decorated pottery beakers, or drinking cups, arrived from the continent of Europe. The Beaker people mined tin in the West Country and traded it on the continent. They put thousands of people to work enlarging Stonehenge.

Starting about 700 B.C., another group of people began to cross the channel. Called Celts (pronounced KELTS), they are the ancestors of the Highland Scots, the Irish, and the Welsh. The Celts were farmers who cleared a great deal of land. They had strong chieftains who built forts. But these forts were not strong enough to withstand the Roman armies, who had taken over much of Europe.

At Flag Fen Bronze Age Centre, reconstructed huts show how people lived three thousand years ago.

Roman Britannia

England's recorded history begins with the Roman Empire. Julius Caesar, emperor of Rome, first conquered France and then twice tried to invade and conquer Great Britain. Each time, his troops were beaten back. A century later, in A.D. 43, another emperor, Claudius, sent troops, and this time they succeeded. During their first century in Great Britain, the Romans built two walls across northern England to prevent raids by northern tribes.

Some tribes in England submitted easily to the Romans. Others did not. When the Iceni tribe's king died, the Romans grabbed his property and had his queen, Boudicca, whipped. Furious, the powerful woman rallied her own soldiers and led them to Londinium (now London), which she burned to the ground. The Romans retaliated by killing many more Iceni men, women, and children.

Roman armies first invaded Great Britain in 55 B.C.

For almost four hundred years, England was the Britannia province of the Roman Empire. People moved from other

Picts
North Sea
Antonine Wall
Picts
Hadrian's Wall
Cataractonium (Catterick)
Brigantes
Eboracum (York)
Hibernia (Ireland)
Irish Sea
Deva (Chester)
Lindum (Lincoln)
Ratae Coritanorum (Leicester)
Ordovices
Corieltavi
Iceni
Catuvellauni
Camulodunum (Colchester)
Glevum (Gloucester)
Verulamium (St. Albans)
Silures
Isca (Caerleon)
Oxford
Londinium (London)
Corinum (Cirencester)
Atrebates
Celtic Sea
Dobuni
Durovernum (Canterbury)
Hinton St. Mary
Belgae
Durotriges
Noviomagus Regnensium (Chichester)
Dumnonii
Isca (Exeter)
English Channel
Roman Conquest of Britain
Roman control, A.D. 43–47
Roman control, A.D. 49–78
Roman control, A.D. 79
Roman control, A.D. 80
Defensive wall
Fort
Settlement
Iceni Tribe

Roman provinces to England. Soldiers brought their families and settled, or they married local women and gradually merged with the Celts. Many camps were established; the English towns with "cester" or "chester" in their names developed from Roman camps. Romans lived well, using slave labor. The first black people in Britain were brought by the Romans.

Rome called its soldiers back home starting in about A.D. 400. But many of them were from families that had lived in Britannia for several generations. They knew nothing about Rome. Rather than go back to an unknown world, they stayed and became British.

Anglo-Saxons and Vikings

After the Romans withdrew from England, little was recorded over the next several centuries. During the fifth and sixth centuries, invaders from northern Europe streamed across the channel and the North Sea. They were primarily from three Germanic tribes—the Saxons, the Angles, and the Jutes. They gradually took control of the island as far north as the Firth of Forth in Scotland and southwest to Cornwall.

"England" did not start until the various tribes began to speak one language and develop one culture, called Anglo-Saxon. During the sixth and seventh centuries, small kingdoms joined forces, usually by marriage, until only three great kingdoms remained—Northumbria, Mercia, and Wessex. Then new trouble arrived. The Norsemen, or Vikings, were invaders from Scandinavia, the part of northern Europe where Norway and Denmark now sit.

About 840, the Vikings began to move across England, destroying villages and church property in order to steal their wealth. They took control of most of central England, a region they called the Danelaw. The first real opposition to the Norse came from Alfred, king of the West Saxons, or Wessex, who ruled from 871. He and his successors gradually took back the Danelaw, and Alfred became known as Alfred the Great.

In 927, Athelstan, the king of Wessex and Mercia, also became king of parts of Northumbria. This united the kingdom of England. Cornwall, whose Celtic people had long fought off the Anglo-Saxons, became part of Athelstan's unified kingdom in 936.

Invasions of Britain

- Danelaw, 912
- Invasion routes
- Wessex, 912
- Battle

In this painting, King Alfred's men are fighting the Vikings in a battle in 897.

The Last Invasion

The last time England was invaded was the year 1066, in an event called the Norman Conquest. The Normans (originally the name meant "Norsemen") were people from a small kingdom called Normandy, now part of France.

The English king at the time was Edward the Confessor, who was more interested in the church than in government or families. He left no children to inherit the throne. Harold Godwin, an Anglo-Saxon earl, claimed the throne, but Duke William of Normandy, a distant cousin of Edward's, wanted England.

The Bayeux Tapestry is a 230-foot-long (70 m long) piece of cloth that tells the story of the Norman Conquest of England. In this scene, William the Conqueror kills King Harold.

From Fort to Tourist Attraction

After defeating England, William the Conqueror built a fort on the north bank of the river Thames, in London. The first building, called the White Tower (shown here), was begun in 1078. Over the following centuries, William's fort grew to become a castle with new outer walls and more towers. In time, the whole complex came to be called the Tower of London. The Tower of London was both a safe place for England's monarchs to stay and a prison for traitors. Today, the tower is popular with tourists and is still protected by guards called Beefeaters, who wear colorful red uniforms that date to the 1500s. The Crown Jewels, which include the crowns of former kings and queens as well as that of the present monarch, are on display in the tower's Jewel House.

William invaded England and triumphed over Harold's army at the Battle of Hastings. William the Conqueror was crowned king of England on Christmas Day, 1066.

When William died in 1087, one of his sons, William Rufus, became king. Rufus was disliked, mainly because he demanded high taxes. When he was killed while hunting—in what may or may not have been an accident—his youngest son became Henry I. But when Henry died in 1135, it was unclear who should ascend to the throne. There was much fighting within the family until 1154, when Henry II began his rule.

Henry II was furious that Thomas Becket supported the church over the kingdom. The king is said to have shouted, "Who will rid me of this meddlesome priest?" and Becket was soon killed.

Henry II is considered one of the best kings of the era. He improved administration throughout the kingdom. He also improved the legal system, introducing trial by jury. These changes took power away from the courts run by the Roman Catholic Church. This angered Henry's old friend Thomas Becket, the archbishop of Canterbury. Becket made decisions based on the idea that the church was superior to the king. The king wanted to get rid of Becket. Four of his knights murdered the archbishop in Canterbury Cathedral. Thomas Becket was declared a saint by the pope, the head of the church in Rome.

Henry's oldest son, Richard, called the Lion-Hearted, became king in 1189. But he spent most of his adult life in the Middle East fighting the religious wars called the Crusades rather than ruling England. When he died abroad, his brother John became king. John soon lost most of England's land in France. He also got into a dispute with the church. Both of these problems angered the barons, the noblemen who had pledged allegiance to the king. On June 15, 1215, the barons demanded that he meet them in a field at Runnymede near London. They forced him to sign a document guaranteeing that the king would, like any citizen, submit to law. In modified form, it became the famed *Magna Carta*, or "the Great Charter," a document that has influenced constitutions through the ages, including the U.S. Constitution.

King John signed the Magna Carta in 1215. He died the following year.

Beginning in 1337, England faced more than a hundred years of on-and-off war with France. This tested the willingness of the English people to pay taxes for the various kings' desires to regain French land. The war dragged on, and battles went against the English. They finally gave up their claim to French lands in 1453.

By the time the Hundred Years' War ended, two men were competing for the throne of England: Henry VI, a descendant of the Duke of Lancaster, and Richard, Duke of York. The Lancastrian symbol was a red rose, while the Yorkists were

The Hundred Years' War actually lasted 116 years. Many of its battles were fought in France.

The ruins of Sandal Castle, the one-time home of Richard, Duke of York. He was killed there during the Battle of Wakefield in 1460.

symbolized by a white rose. The power struggle became a civil war, which is called the War of the Roses. The war lasted more than thirty-five years. It finally ended in 1485, when Richard III, the last Yorkist king, was killed on the battlefield by Henry Tudor, a Lancastrian. Henry Tudor became Henry VII and wed the daughter of the Yorkist king Edward IV. He thus united the red rose and the white, forming a new royal house—the Tudors.

Building the United Kingdom

Henry VII came from a Welsh family. England had long had trouble with the Welsh, who sometimes made raids from the west. In 1284, in an effort to keep the Welsh friendly, Edward I had declared his son to be Prince of Wales. Ever since, most English monarchs have given their male heirs this title. More than two hundred years later, in 1536, Henry VII's son, Henry VIII, finally united the two countries.

The English had been on the island of Ireland since the thirteenth century. But it wasn't until 1541 that Henry VIII forced the Irish to acknowledge him as their king. Henry VIII had broken with the Roman Catholic Church, establishing a Protestant church called the Church of England in its place. Henry tried to make the Irish become Protestant, but with little success. Rebellions and anger developed over the fact that Catholics had few political rights. In the twentieth century, the southern two-thirds of the island of Ireland broke away from the United Kingdom and became the independent nation called the Republic of Ireland. Northern Ireland remains part of the United Kingdom.

The English spent centuries trying to conquer Scotland so that they could control the entire island of Great Britain. When Queen Elizabeth I died in 1603 without an heir, King James VI of Scotland, her cousin, became king of England. The countries were finally united by the Act of Union in 1707.

The German artist Hans Holbein the Younger painted this portrait of Henry VIII.

Building an Empire

Elizabeth was the third child of Henry VIII to become monarch. The first was Edward VI, who ascended to the throne in

1547 at age nine. Edward died as a teenager, and his older half sister, Mary, became queen. A Roman Catholic, Mary ruled only long enough to become known as "Bloody Mary" for executing many Protestants. Her younger sister, Elizabeth, a Protestant, turned England into a strongly Protestant nation.

During Elizabeth's reign, English power began to extend around the world. Sir Walter Raleigh, one of the queen's advisers, tried to start colonies in what is now Virginia. In the 1570s, Francis Drake became the first Englishman to sail around the world. Drake also attacked Spanish ships coming from South America, stealing their gold. His raids, as well as the Spaniards' staunch Catholicism, prompted Spain to send a great fleet of ships—an armada—to invade England.

Spanish and English forces face off in 1588. After the defeat of the Spanish Armada, many English people felt confident about their place as a world power.

In 1588, 130 Spanish ships set out for England. But the men had few provisions, and powerful winds slowed their passage. They were attacked by the English navy on their way up the English Channel, and then a storm destroyed many of the ships. After the defeat of the Spanish Armada, the English believed that they were the greatest sailors on earth and had the greatest navy.

Without Parliament, Without a King

Since about 1200, an advisory council called Parliament had been active in England. Sometimes the king paid attention to it, and sometimes he didn't. When King James VI of Scotland became King James I of England, he went to London with one firm idea: He was king by "divine right" and did not have to listen to Parliament. He passed this same attitude on to his son, Charles I. Charles dismissed Parliament and ruled until civil war between Parliament and the king broke out in 1642.

Parliament's army, led by Oliver Cromwell, beheaded Charles in 1649. Cromwell, who called himself Lord Protector, ran the country until his death in 1658. He was a Protestant Puritan, who hated Catholicism and believed that the Church of England needed "purifying"

Oliver Cromwell leads his troops in battle during the English Civil War. Though he had no military training, Cromwell became a talented commander who led disciplined forces.

to become simpler. Puritans wanted less ritual and more Bible reading and prayer.

After Cromwell's death, the people demanded that the monarchy be restored. Charles I's son, Charles II, was called to become king. Problems with the monarchy continued, however. The next king, James II, was so pro-Catholic that Parliament asked James II's daughter, Mary, a Protestant, and her husband, Prince William of Orange, to come from the Netherlands and rule England jointly. James fled, and William and Mary ruled under strict guidelines that turned England into a constitutional monarchy.

William of Orange led an invasion of England that is sometimes called the Glorious Revolution. William and his wife, Mary, served as joint monarchs.

Rapid Change

In the coming centuries, England would become more embroiled in events around the world. In the 1600s and 1700s, English colonies were set up all along the east coast

The Great Fire

In 1666, four-fifths of the City of London was destroyed by the Great Fire, which burned for four days. The fire burned 13,200 houses and 87 churches to the ground.

Architect Sir Christopher Wren designed replacements for most of the churches destroyed in the fire, including St. Paul's Cathedral.

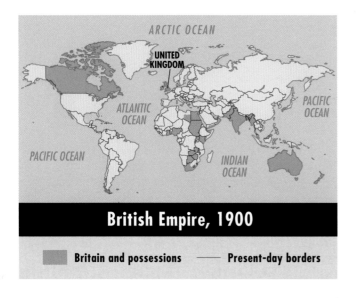

British Empire, 1900

Britain and possessions —— Present-day borders

of North America. George III was king of England when the American colonies declared their independence in 1776.

The American Revolution was hardly over when England was thrown into another war, this time mostly on the continent. The Napoleonic Wars, named after the French general Napoleon Bonaparte, raged for twenty years. These wars ended in 1815, when the troops of England's Duke of Wellington beat Napoleon at the Battle of Waterloo in Belgium. With this triumph, England emerged as the most powerful nation on earth. By this time, Britain had already begun establishing colonies from Australia to India to Africa. It was said that "the sun never sets on the British Empire" because it had colonies all around the world.

The Battle of Waterloo, 1815, **painted by William Allen. Historians estimate that nearly fifty thousand men died in the battle.**

The Industrial Revolution had begun in England in the mid-1700s. Mills and factories sprung up across the nation. Railroads and canals were built to quickly move goods around. Almost overnight, England quickly changed from an agricultural country to an industrial one. But these changes brought many problems. Workers, including some children as young as five, labored long hours in mines and factories. And the working class lacked adequate housing. Sometimes, dozens of people would sleep crowded together in one small room.

Child labor was common in the 1800s in England. In 1833, Parliament limited the number of hours children under nine could work in textile mills. This was an early small step toward ending child labor in England.

Gradually, though, laws were passed to keep children from hard labor. In 1833, a law banned children under age nine from working. Children from nine to eighteen could work no more than twelve hours a day. Trade unions also began to organize for workers' rights. Schools were established for the nation's children. In 1837, England gained a new queen, Victoria. She would rule until 1901 and would give her name to the Victorian era, a time in England of great prosperity for the elite and great poverty for the underclasses.

The World at War

England found itself frequently at war in the first half of the twentieth century. Twice, Germany tried to take over neighboring countries. Both times, Britain led other nations in an effort to stop Germany. World War I began for England in 1914, when its soldiers had to go to the European continent to help France. The war ended in 1918, after the United States sent in troops to help. But by that time, 750,000 British soldiers had died. The war had cost so much that England was no longer the world's mightiest nation.

Twenty years after World War I ended, World War II (1939–1945) began as Germany once again tried to expand its borders, this time under the brutal Nazi leader Adolf Hitler. After conquering France, the Germans began to attack England. For two months in 1940, British pilots took their fighter planes into the air to prevent German bombers from destroying Britain's air force and other targets. Gradually, this "Battle of Britain" paid off. Hitler decided he could not invade.

But he could still bomb the country. For months, Germany dropped bombs on London and nearby towns in what came to be called the Blitz. Londoners spent long, frightening nights underground in subway stations. They emerged each morning to find more of London flattened.

Soon, almost every nation in the world was involved in the war. England, under Prime Minister Winston Churchill, became the staging area for troops to invade the continent and fight Hitler on his own ground. Huge numbers of troops from the United States, Canada, Australia, and many other nations crossed the channel from England in June 1944. Within months, Hitler was defeated.

Smoke streams over London during the Blitz. More than a million houses were destroyed during the bombing campaign.

The long war left Britain unable to support its many colonies. In 1947, the United Kingdom granted India independence after a long struggle led by Mahatma Gandhi, who inspired millions with his call for nonviolent protest. Over the next two decades, other British colonies from Kenya to Malaysia also gained their independence.

To the Present

In the 1970s and 1980s, England faced great economic trouble. Manufacturing went into decline and there were many labor strikes. Conservative Margaret Thatcher was prime minister throughout the 1980s. She cut government spending, broke labor unions, and sold off government industries. By the time she left office in 1990, she was deeply unpopular.

Margaret Thatcher, First Woman Prime Minister

Margaret Roberts was born in Lincolnshire in 1925. While studying chemistry at Oxford University, she joined the Conservative Party. She believed that the government should not be involved in people's lives. After leaving Oxford, she married Denis Thatcher, a businessman. She then studied to become a lawyer and became more active in Conservative politics.

In 1959, Margaret Thatcher was elected to Parliament. Working her way up through various party positions, she was elected to head the party in 1975. When the Conservatives won the election of 1979, she, as head of the party, became prime minister. She held that position until 1990. By that time, she'd become very unpopular. Her uncompromising positions earned her the name nickname "the Iron Lady."

In 1997, Tony Blair of the Labour Party became prime minister. Since then, the United Kingdom has sided closely with the United States. When terrorists destroyed the World Trade Center in New York on September 11, 2001, Blair said that the people of Britain "stand shoulder to shoulder with our American friends." He supported U.S. president George W. Bush's decision to invade Iraq in 2003 to topple dictator Saddam Hussein. The English people, however, did not support the war, and Blair's popularity dropped.

On July 6, 2005, the English were thrilled to learn that London had been chosen to host the Olympic Games in 2012. But the celebration ended abruptly the next day when terrorists bombed three subways and a bus. More than fifty people were killed. A Muslim terrorist group based in the city of Leeds had carried out the attacks to protest British participation in the war in Iraq. Their joy had turned to grief, but the English knew they had to move forward, as they always have.

Police guard a London subway entrance following the terrorist bombings on July 7, 2005. Bombs ripped apart three subway trains within a minute of each other during the morning rush hour.

Royalty and Parliament

THE UNITED KINGDOM DOES NOT HAVE A WRITTEN CONSTI-
tution like that of the United States. Instead, it has hundreds
of years of custom, development, and law.

At the heart of the United Kingdom's government is
the monarch—the king or queen. Since 1952, the monarch
has been Queen Elizabeth II. The queen lives primarily at
Buckingham Palace in London, but Windsor Castle has been
the official royal residence since the twelfth century. Over the
centuries, some people have complained about taxpayers supporting the royal family, since they are major landowners and
have considerable income from their land. As a result of these
complaints, the queen now pays income taxes.

Opposite: **Queen Elizabeth gives a speech at the opening of Parliament in 2004.**

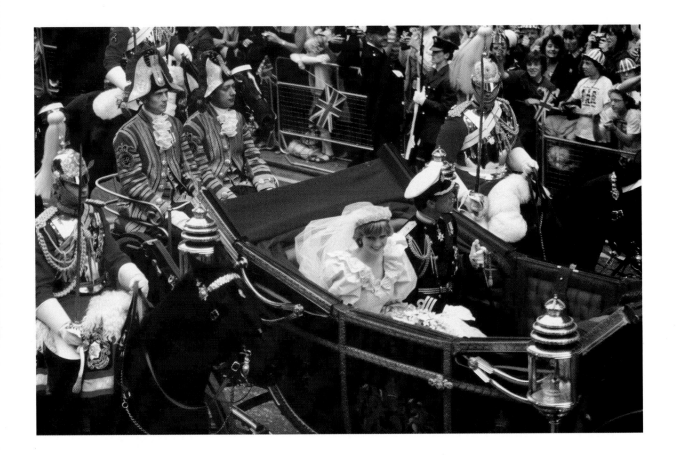

Charles and Diana ride through London on their wedding day in 1981. Their wedding was broadcast on television around the world.

Queen Elizabeth's oldest son, Charles, Prince of Wales, is the heir to the throne. Charles and his wife, Princess Diana, were divorced in 1996. Diana, who was killed in a car crash in 1997, was immensely popular. After Diana's death, Queen Elizabeth admitted that the princess had been popular for a reason—Diana did not remain aloof from the people. Since the monarchy has little actual power, the queen saw that it was going to have to change if it was to survive. The monarchy was going to have to become friendlier and more in touch with the public.

The National Anthem of the United Kingdom

The United Kingdom's national anthem, "God Save the Queen," was first performed publicly in 1745. But the song actually dates to the 1600s or even earlier. No one knows who wrote the words or music. Typically, only the first verse is sung.

God save our gracious Queen,
Long live our noble Queen,
God save the Queen.
Send her victorious,
Happy and glorious,
Long to reign over us:
God save the Queen.

O Lord our God, arise,
Scatter our enemies,
And make them fall;
Confound their politics,
Frustrate their knavish tricks;
On thee our hopes we fix:
God save us all.

Thy choicest gifts in store
On her be pleased to pour,
Long may she reign.
May she defend our laws,
And ever give us cause
To sing with heart and voice,
God save the Queen.

Not in this land alone,
But be God's mercies known,
From shore to shore!
Lord make the nations see,
That men should brothers be,
And form one family,
The wide world over.

From every latent foe,
From the assassins blow,
God save the Queen!
O'er her thine arm extend,
For Britain's sake defend,
Our mother, prince, and friend,
God save the Queen!

The Next Heir to the Throne

Though Prince Charles is the heir to the throne, many people want his son Prince William to become the next king. William was born in 1982. He attended the elite boarding school called Eton. Like many English students, he took a year off before starting university. During that time, he traveled the world. He then studied geography at St. Andrews University in Scotland, graduating with honors in 2005. The following year he began training to be an army officer.

NATIONAL GOVERNMENT OF ENGLAND

The Queen

Executive Branch

PRIME MINISTER

CABINET OF MINISTERS

Legislative Branch

NATIONAL ASSEMBLY

HOUSE OF LORDS   HOUSE OF COMMONS

Judicial Branch

COURT OF APPEAL

CROWN COURT

MAGISTRATES

Moving Power to Parliament

At times throughout history, the monarchs in various countries held absolute power—the power to do whatever they wanted. This was not so in the United Kingdom. The power of the monarch was limited long ago by the powers of Parliament. England's Parliament has been meeting for more than seven hundred years.

Parliament is made up of two parts, the House of Lords and the House of Commons. For centuries, the House of Lords,

the upper house, consisted of the bishops of the Church of England and titled people such as knights, barons, and earls. These wealthy landowners are also called hereditary peers; they pass their titles on to their children. In recent years, life peerages were created. People such as industrialists and actors are given titles in honor of their achievements. These titles do not pass to their children. In 1970, famed actor Laurence Olivier became the first actor be given a life peerage.

The House of Lords hasn't really functioned as an important legislative body since 1911 when it lost the right to reject laws passed by the House of Commons. In 1999, an act of Parliament began to reform the House of Lords. Hereditary peers no longer automatically got seats. Until further changes are made, 92 hereditary peers were named to join the 552 life peers to keep the House of Lords functioning.

The House of Lords meets in a lavish room in the Houses of Parliament. The members of the House of Lords sit on the red benches along the sides.

Flags and Dragons

The Union Jack—a flag of red, white, and blue with a red cross through the center—is the official flag of the United Kingdom. England itself has no official flag, but the flag called St. George's Cross has been used for centuries. It consists of the red cross and white background of the Union Jack.

Saint George is the patron saint of England. He was a Roman soldier who lived around A.D. 300. He was persecuted for becoming Christian. Popular legend says that Saint George slew a dragon, perhaps near the town of Glastonbury, although there is no evidence that he was ever in England—or that England ever had real dragons.

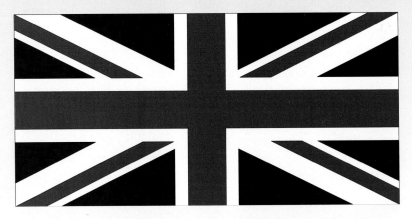

Members of the House of Commons are elected. Today, there are 659 members of Parliament, called MPs, in the House of Commons, with 529 of them from England. There are currently two main political parties—the Conservative Party and the Labour Party. The head of the political party that wins the most seats becomes the prime minister of the United Kingdom. The prime minister must appear in Parliament regularly to answer questions. These sessions can become quite noisy because politeness is not expected.

Elections must be held at least every five years, but they are often more frequent. A new election has to be held if the prime minister loses an important "vote of confidence," which says he or she can no longer hold the position. Unlike elections in the United States, where a presidential election campaign can last a year or more, British elections usually take place within six weeks of being announced. Any citizen at least eighteen years old can vote.

Beyond Parliament

The executive branch of the British government is made up of the ministers, or department heads, who are named by the prime minister. Ministers must be members of the House of Commons. Most ministers are members of the cabinet, the group that works most closely with the prime minister. Ministers are also members of the Privy Council, which is the council of advisers to the monarch.

Prime Minister Tony Blair (second from left) walks with members of his cabinet. Most cabinet members belong to the House of Commons.

The judiciary is under the control of the lord chancellor, a member of the House of Lords. England and Wales have one legal system, while Scotland and Northern Ireland have their own systems. In England, the Crown Court hears very serious cases, such as murder and treason. Juries hear all cases before the Crown Court. Less serious cases are heard by magistrates without juries. A case heard by a magistrate can be appealed to the Crown Court, and a Crown Court case can be appealed to the Court of Appeal. The final Court of Appeal is the House of Lords, but only if the case involves an important principle of law.

London's Kingston Crown Court is one of the more than ninety crown courts spread across England and Wales.

England has thirty-nine separate police forces. The police force often called Scotland Yard is actually the Metropolitan Police of London. The name comes from the location of the original building, where important visitors from Scotland stayed centuries ago. The name stuck, even when the police moved into new buildings. Scotland Yard can be called in by any of the other police forces if they need help solving a case.

England is known as a law-abiding country, where social politeness is important. But in recent years, violent crime has become more widespread in Britain. Theft is common, but murder is still relatively rare. The English think this is because guns are rare. Even the police carry guns only under unusual circumstances, such as when bombs were set off on London subways and buses in 2005.

Scotland Yard is now located in a twenty-story building near the Houses of Parliament.

London's city hall opened in 2002. Some people call it the glass egg. It is the office of the mayor of London and seat of the twenty-five-member Greater London Assembly.

Governing Beyond London

Many residents of Scotland and Wales have long hoped that they would gain the right to rule their own regions of the United Kingdom. Finally in 1999, the Scottish Parliament and the Welsh Assembly were established. England itself does not have a governing body separate from the government of the United Kingdom.

In the United Kingdom, counties are the traditional level of local government. But London also has the Greater London Assembly, which coordinates regional policy for more than seven million residents of the area.

Being Part of Europe

After World War II, which left large parts of Europe in ruins, some people called for European nations to unite in ways that would benefit them all. Closed borders between countries would be opened. The nations would join together as an economic force that could compete with the United States, Japan, and other major trading countries. The UK officially became a member of this organization of nations, called the Common Market, in 1973.

By 2005, the name had changed to the European Union (EU). The organization currently has twenty-five member nations, including the United Kingdom. The EU nations have become more and more integrated economically, socially, and politically. Each nation sends representatives to the increasingly important European Parliament. The member states also send representatives to institutions such as the EU Commission and the European Court of Justice.

EU decisions affect all the member states. Some of these decisions have been relatively easy for the English to accept. When the EU decided that all the countries involved should use the metric system, British businesses gradually switched. But in other areas, England is reluctant to let itself come under the control of other nations. For example, the English don't want the EU to control immigration. And they refused to adopt the euro, the common currency that many EU countries began using in 2002.

The European Parliament meets in Brussels, Belgium. Each country in the European Union sends between six and ninety-six members to Parliament.

London: Did You Know This?

London was founded by the Romans as Londinium. It started as a village that grew up around the first wooden bridge to span the river Thames. The Romans eventually built a wall around the city, probably to protect themselves. The wall also kept the village from growing large. Today, the 1-square-mile (2.6 sq km) area within the wall is the City of London. It's the old financial heart of the city.

For many centuries, the only way to cross the Thames was by boat or by taking the Old London Bridge (famous for "falling down"). Built in 1176 with houses and shops along its length, the London Bridge lasted more than 650 years. Today, many bridges cross the Thames.

Theaters, shops, restaurants, museums, hotels, and the government are amazingly close together in

central London. But the crowding is broken up by major parks. Hyde Park and Kensington Gardens make up the biggest green area. Buckingham Palace is located next to Green Park and St. James's Park. Regent's Park contains the famed London Zoo. Hampstead Heath is a huge natural area with lakes, woods, and shrubs.

London's West End has many squares, often with grass and trees, which help break up the crowded feel of the big city. The British Museum stands in Russell Square. Trafalgar Square (above right) is a place where everyone meets. It is graced by the National Gallery. Leicester Square is known for its theaters.

A giant Ferris wheel stands on the South Bank of the river Thames opposite the Houses of Parliament. Called the London Eye, it carries sightseers in thirty-two enclosed capsules 443 feet (135 m) high to view the spectacular city of London from above.

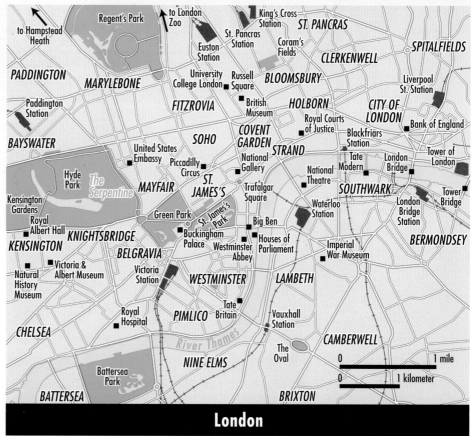

London

Industry and
Business

B RITAIN WAS THE WORLD'S FIRST INDUSTRIALIZED NATION, meaning it was the first to have an economy based on industry rather than agriculture. Between 1760 and 1830, the English economy and society changed greatly. Similar changes soon happened across the globe.

Opposite: **The Quarry Bank Mill began producing cloth in 1784. Today, it is a living museum, where visitors can see how cloth was once made.**

Farming and Fishing

Long before the Industrial Revolution, England's wealth depended on the gentleness of its climate. Farmers could count on their crops growing, and there was plenty of land for grazing livestock, especially sheep for wool. Today, only 2 percent of the workforce is involved in agriculture, forestry, or fishing. Less than 1 percent of the nation's economy depends on farming, though 77 percent of the land is used for agriculture.

The Cotswold Lion

The Cotswold lion is a breed of sheep with a shaggy coat. The Cotswolds are beautiful limestone uplands in southwestern England. The Cotswold lion, which has long, fast-growing fleece, was developed there. In fact, the name *Cotswold* means "sheep hills."

The major crops grown in England are wheat, barley, potatoes, and sugar beets. England also produces a great deal of rapeseed, a plant that produces both canola oil used in cooking and an oil that can be used as part of diesel fuel.

Most agricultural land in England is grass pasture used to graze cattle and sheep. In the 1990s, many British cattle

The potato, which is native to Central and South America, was first brought to England in the late 1500s. Today, potatoes are one of England's leading crops.

contracted a terrible illness called mad cow disease. When it was found that the disease could be passed to people, thousands of cows had to be killed. Their bodies were then burned. Today, the disease is much less common in England because of rigorous inspections.

The English are big fish eaters. Both sole and flounder are caught in the English Channel. The main catches off other parts of England include mackerel, herring, and cod. England has long had a major fishing fleet. But overfishing has harmed the industry, and now fewer fishing boats head out from British ports.

Worldwide Industries

England has long been known for its research into medical drugs, or pharmaceuticals. A Scotsman named Alexander Fleming, working in England, discovered penicillin. This was the first antibiotic, a drug that can kill the germs that cause some diseases. Today, the English own the largest pharmaceutical company in the world, GlaxoSmithKlein.

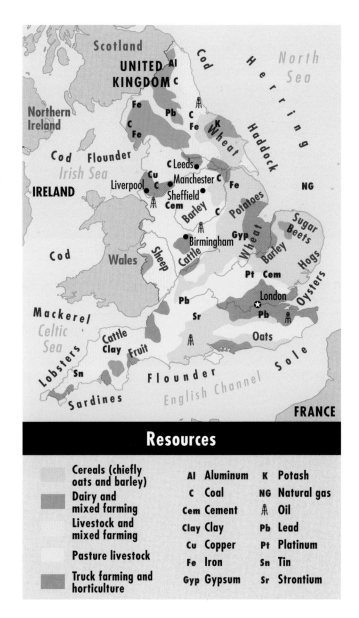

Resources

Cereals (chiefly oats and barley)	**Al** Aluminum	**K** Potash
Dairy and mixed farming	**C** Coal	**NG** Natural gas
Livestock and mixed farming	**Cem** Cement	**Oil**
Pasture livestock	**Clay** Clay	**Pb** Lead
	Cu Copper	**Pt** Platinum
Truck farming and horticulture	**Fe** Iron	**Sn** Tin
	Gyp Gypsum	**Sr** Strontium

A worker decorates a plate at the Royal Doulton Factory.

England is also known for its fine porcelain, or bone china. In about 1800, English manufacturers learned to make strong but delicate, almost transparent, dishes from bone ash and clay found mostly in the West Country. Spode and Royal Doulton are two big manufacturers of bone china. Josiah Wedgwood popularized Jasperware, beautiful pottery with white raised figures on a blue background.

Flying High

Richard Branson is a man of many interests. He got his start in business at age nineteen selling records by mail order. Soon he had formed his own record label called Virgin Records, which recorded some hugely popular groups such as the Sex Pistols and the Rolling Stones. This led him to open music stores called Virgin Megastores, which are now found all over the world.

Branson has expanded his business in many directions. He runs an airline called Virgin Atlantic. He also owns rail lines, bridal shops, bike rentals, wineries, health clubs, and an international cell-phone company. He has said, "I want Virgin to be as well known around the world as Coca-Cola."

Branson is a personal adventurer, too. He became the first person to cross the Atlantic Ocean in a hot-air balloon in 1987. He then repeated the feat across the Pacific Ocean. He tried to fly a balloon around the world, but was not successful. He has recently started a commercial space-flight business and is selling tickets to ride into space.

What the United Kingdom Grows, Makes, and Mines

Agriculture

Wheat	14,288,000 metric tons
Sugar beets	9,296,000 metric tons
Potatoes	5,918,000 metric tons

Manufacturing

Food and beverages	76,700,000,000
Electrical equipment	53,100,000,000
Transportation equipment	46,400,000,000

Mining

Oil	2.4 million barrels/day
Limestone	93,600,000 metric tons
Sand and gravel	94,400,000 metric tons

Bentley has been making luxury cars at Crewe since 1946.

British Aerospace, an aircraft company, works with other European firms on the Airbus. This group is now developing the world's biggest airliner, an Airbus that will carry 550 people. Rolls-Royce, best known for its very special—and very expensive—cars, is also the world's third-largest manufacturer of airplane engines. Other luxury cars such as the Jaguar and the Bentley are also made in England.

Service Industries

Though England has a strong history of farming and manufacturing, about 70 percent of the English economy is made up of service industries. These include such things as real estate, health care, tourism, education, and trade. The City of London, the oldest part of London, is a worldwide financial center. It is the site of many banks, the London Stock Exchange, and Lloyd's of London, one of the world's most famous insurance companies.

A Nation of Shopkeepers

England was once called "a nation of shopkeepers." The main street (called "the high street") in every town and city has small shops that sell items such as candy, newspapers, ice

England's Money

England's (and the United Kingdom's) currency is called the pound sterling. For centuries, the pound was divided into twenty shillings, with twelve pennies, or pence, to the shilling. There were also half-penny coins and quarter-penny coins called farthings. A large five-shilling coin was called a crown. A smaller coin worth two shillings and sixpence was a half crown. An amount called a guinea represented one pound, one shilling

Except for the pound (whose symbol is £), these coins no longer exist. In 1971, the old monetary system was changed to a decimal system. The pound remained the same, but it is now worth 100 pence, abbreviated p. When

saying a price, the people say, for example, that a candy bar costs "50 p." In 2006, one pound was worth 1.77 U.S. dollars.

cream, meats, bread, and milk. During the 1980s and 1990s, shopping in England became more like American shopping. Today, many people buy their groceries in supermarkets. Malls are now found on the outskirts of towns. As in the United States, such shopping centers have sometimes hurt business in the high streets.

In 1999, Europe's largest shopping center and recreation complex opened in Greenhithe, in Kent. Called Bluewater, its parklike setting, including a large lake, covers 240 acres (100 hectares). The mall has been attracting twenty-seven million shoppers a year since it opened.

A Great Way to Shop

Some towns still have markets where people with something to sell set up carts on market day. One of the most famous streets in London is Petticoat Lane. This is not actually the name of the street. Instead, it is a nickname for Middlesex Street, the centuries-old site of a second-hand clothing market. Today, Petticoat Lane sells anything that a dealer, or "pitchman," wants to sell. Equally famous is a similar market called Portobello Road in the Notting Hill area. Such markets are worth a visit.

England has had a few small oil wells over the years, but the amount of oil pumped was insignificant compared to the gigantic North Sea oil field discovered off the east coast of Scotland in the 1960s. Today, oil is pumped from more than sixty offshore wells. Most of that oil makes its way through pipelines to England, where it is burned as fuel and used in manufacturing petrochemicals.

Underneath parts of northern and central England lie huge beds of coal that were mined in the eighteenth and nineteenth centuries to feed the furnaces of the Industrial Revolution. Even in the twentieth century, coal mines were still functioning, but today only eight deep mines are still being worked. There are another ten open mines, with more in Scotland. Coal produces about 35 percent of the nation's electricity.

The world's first commercial nuclear power plant was built in England at Calder Hall in Cumbria. It began supplying electricity to customers in 1956. Today, about 22 percent of England's electricity comes from its twelve nuclear power plants.

An oil platform rises above the waters of the North Sea. The United Kingdom produces about two million barrels of oil every day.

In the future, England plans to emphasize wind power. Groups of wind mills, called wind farms, are being built both on land and offshore. The first large-scale offshore wind farm, located at North Hoyle, began operating in 2003.

Labor and Industry

In 1900, the labor unions created the Labour Party in England. They won a majority in Parliament for the first time in 1924, and their leader, Ramsey MacDonald, became prime minister. The Labour Party believed that the government should run as many industries as possible, so that workers could be guaranteed their jobs. They were also the first to support government-sponsored health programs and other social services.

Starting after World War II, the Labour government took over, or nationalized, many major businesses in England. At first, the industries were run more efficiently than they had been with private owners. Over the years, however, the nationalized industries became less profitable and less efficient.

At the same time as industry was nationalized, the medical services of England were also nationalized. Most doctors work for the National Health Service (NHS) rather than for themselves or a hospital. More than a million people work for the NHS, making it one of the largest employers in the world.

When Margaret Thatcher became prime minister in 1979, the Conservative government began to return nationalized businesses to private ownership. British Aerospace was among the first companies to go private. The telephone company, British Telecom, has been private since 1984. In 1993,

British Rail was broken up into twenty-five different regions. Different companies gained the right to run the trains in the different regions.

The Cost of Being Upper Class

Traditionally in England, upper-class families owned large estates. It was important that family estates not be broken up, because that's where the family wealth lay.

These estates relied on cheap farm labor. But after World War II, farming income dropped because cheap labor was no longer available. The owners of these large estates had to find ways to take care of the houses and pay taxes on the land. Many chose to open the houses to the public. Tourists pay a fee to walk through the historic rooms. Some large houses have been turned into hotels, schools, or offices.

Some estate owners have used imaginative ways to keep their estates in the family. In 1970, the Duke of Bedford, who owns Woburn Abbey, opened Safari Country, a drive-through park with wild animals. Woburn Abbey has been so successful at breeding endangered animals that fifty Père David's deer have been sent back to China, where they had been extinct for more than a hundred years. The four-hundred-year-old house at Beaulieu Abbey (left) features the National Motor Museum. It has one of the most complete collections of historic cars in the world. Longleat House in Wiltshire, owned by the Marquess of Bath, features England's largest maze. Visitors can ramble along more than 1.5 miles (2.4 km) of trails, hoping to find their way out again.

London has more than seven hundred different bus routes. On workdays, about six million people ride London's buses.

Getting Around

England has a system of canals built in the 1700s and 1800s, just before the invention of the steam train. Originally intended for freight, the canals are now used for recreational boating. After 1905, nothing was added to the 2,000-mile (3,200 km) waterway system until a new section near Leeds opened in 1995.

The London bus system has long used the world-famous double-decker red buses. Since 2006, they are being replaced by single-decker buses. Single-deckers also serve districts outside London. The London Underground, which opened in 1863, is the oldest subway system in the world. It runs on 253 miles (408 km) of track in and around London. Parts of the "Tube" are very deep underground. The world's longest escalators carry people back up to street level.

The Great Shipbuilder

Isambard Kingdom Brunel was a Portsmouth-born engineer who built bridges, tunnels, and innovative ships that turned the United Kingdom into a ship-building powerhouse. The *Great Western*, designed by Brunel, was the first steamship to provide regular passenger service across the Atlantic. It was launched in 1837. The *Great Britain*, launched seven years later, was the first steam-powered passenger liner to have an iron hull. This first luxury liner can still be seen in the harbor at Bristol.

Eurostar trains carry passengers under the English Channel from France all the way to Waterloo Station in London.

England is also crisscrossed by railway lines that carry people and goods around the country. For centuries, the only way to cross the English Channel to France was by boat. The invention of the airplane added a second way to get across.

Since 1968, a boat called a hovercraft has carried people—and their cars—across the channel on a cushion of air. But many people also dreamed of a tunnel under the sea that would link England and France for the first time in eight thousand years. The work of building the 31-mile (50 km) Channel Tunnel—often called the Chunnel—began in 1986. The Chunnel opened in 1994. Trains now run through two separate one-way tunnels, carrying people, cars, buses, and freight. The trains are inside the tunnel for just twenty minutes.

London's Heathrow Airport handles well over fifty million passengers every year. Gatwick, also near London, is the second-busiest airport in England. Manchester and Stansted are third and fourth. The combined traffic of these other airports doesn't add up to Heathrow's, which is the busiest airport in Europe and the third-busiest in the world.

Despite all this public transportation, thousands of people drive into London every day, causing terrible traffic jams. The Greater London Assembly tackled this problem in 2003 by establishing a fee of five pounds a day (later raised to eight pounds) for all cars entering central London. It seems to be working, and traffic has improved.

Taking a Chance

The United Kingdom has had a national lottery since 1993. In a lottery, people buy a ticket at a low price with the hope that they will win a large amount of money if their ticket is drawn. There is a lot of money left over from the ticket purchases. Britain has used this extra money to support organizations that it otherwise would not have had money to fund.

Sport England, for example, is committed to helping people get involved in sporting and fitness activities. Its Web site identifies fifteen thousand places in England where people can take part in physical activities. Internationally, British charities that help people in the world's poorest countries are supported by lottery funds.

The English People

FAR BACK IN HISTORY, ENGLAND'S PEOPLE CAME FROM MANY lands. But between the Norman Conquest in 1066 and about 1800, England's residents came together into a nation of people called the English.

Opposite: **A London policeman on the job**

Speaking English

The language spoken by the Anglo-Saxons, now called Old English, developed from the Germanic languages spoken by the invading tribes. Alfred the Great, king of the West Saxons, translated many works from Latin into his own language. A long heroic poem called *Beowulf* was written in Old English about A.D. 700. Some words that survive from Old English are *write*, *oxen*, and *bring*.

Later invaders influenced the language, too. Danish words, brought by Vikings, are important to English, as are French words. This variety of sources gives English perhaps the largest vocabulary of any language.

English did not become the primary language of England's literature until the 1300s, when Geoffrey Chaucer wrote *The Canterbury Tales*. His language is called Middle English. King Henry V made English the official language in the early 1400s. Modern English was fully in use by the 1600s. But the spellings and meanings were not standardized until the eighteenth century, when the first English dictionaries were published.

A page from *The Canterbury Tales*. The tales were written in the 1380s and the 1390s.

Translating English into English

Thousands of words that are common in England have to be "translated" for Americans. Here are some:

jumper = sweater

chemist = drugstore

chips = french fries

come a cropper = end up badly

dual carriageway = divided highway

fortnight = two weeks

gaol = jail (but pronounced the same)

lift = elevator

lorry = truck

not cricket = not fair; not acceptable

nappy = diaper

brilliant = fabulous, wonderful

American English is closer to the English used in the American colonies than it is to the language of today's England. For example, *color* and *favor* were usually spelled without u's three hundred years ago, but the English came to prefer to spell them *colour* and *favour*.

About 380 million people around the world speak English as their first language. Another half billion speak it as a second language.

Both English and Welsh are spoken in areas of England bordering Wales. Many signs in the area display both languages.

Rochester Castle in Kent was one of the first English castles to be made of stone. It was built in about 1090.

Knights, Dukes, and Earls

England has a long tradition of giving titles to the elites in society. Starting with William the Conqueror, the English king named a number of his favorite knights "barons" and gave them great estates. The barons, in turn, gave their favorite knights some land. Each knight was expected to build a castle or fort and to protect the people who lived on his land. This system is called feudalism. In return for land, each knight was expected to serve at the castle of his lord for forty days each year.

Knights could be identified through heraldry—designs, colors, and symbols that represent families. The most common heraldic symbol is the coat of arms, which was worn by a knight dressed in armor for battle. Heraldry developed during the Crusades to help the armored men identify one another.

In the thirteenth century, Edward I invited landowners to attend a parliament to advise him. This was the beginning of the House of Lords. These advisers became earls, a title the Anglo-Saxons had used. Their wives were called countesses.

Edward III created a new rank, called duke, which today is the top rank. A duke's wife is a duchess. Only five dukes belong to the royal family. Between duke and earl is the marquess, a title created in 1385, and below earl is viscount. The lowest categories are baron and baronet.

Commoners sometimes became aristocrats. A man named John Churchill fought King Louis XIV of France so well that Queen Anne made him the Duke of Marlborough. She also gave him a huge palace called Blenheim. Centuries later, a descendant of the Duke of Marlborough, Winston Churchill, served as prime minister during World War II.

In 1295, Edward I met with a parliament that included aristocrats, religious leaders, and representatives from around England. This was the model for what became the British Parliament.

A Variety of People

Between 1800 and 1900, England's population quadrupled. Most of the growth occurred in London and other cities. Today, England has a population density of 150 people per square mile (389 per sq km). That is almost twice the density of Germany and four times that of France. The United Kingdom's population is expected to increase by six million during the next twenty-five years. Most of this increase will come from immigration.

People have never stopped moving to England. In the early 1800s, most immigrants were from Ireland. They took the lowliest jobs available and gradually began to make homes for themselves. Later, thousands of Jews came to London from Russia. They took jobs in tiny workshops for low wages. The shops were often called sweatshops because the conditions were so bad. Over time, the Jews became part of English society. They no longer stood out as a group.

Immigrants began to arrive from the West Indies in 1948. Most were from Jamaica. Soon thereafter, Indians, Pakistanis,

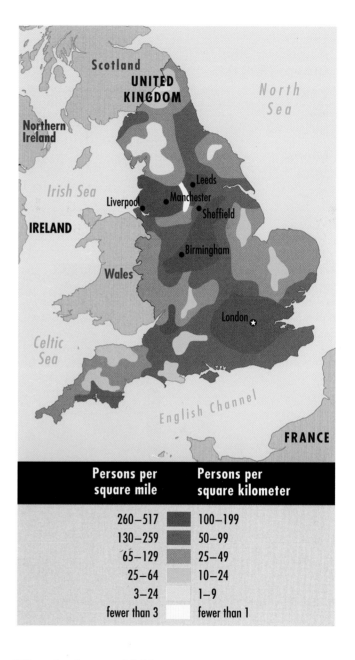

Persons per square mile	Persons per square kilometer
260–517	100–199
130–259	50–99
65–129	25–49
25–64	10–24
3–24	1–9
fewer than 3	fewer than 1

The United Kingdom's Ethnic Groups (2001)

White	92%
Black	2%
Indian	1.8%
Pakistani	1.3%
Mixed	1.2%
Other	1.6%

Racial tensions ran high in England in the early 1980s. In 1981, demonstrators and police clashed in South London.

and Bangladeshis began to arrive. Struggles between the races began in the 1960s. Parliament passed a law in 1968 that let a person immigrate only if he or she had a parent, spouse, or child who was already a citizen. In 1976, another law was passed making racial discrimination illegal in housing, employment, or education. That didn't put an end to racial strife, however. In the 1980s, riots broke out in a number of cities, including the Brixton area of London, over the way the police treated blacks.

More than three hundred thousand followers of the Sikh religion live in England. Many of them immigrated from India.

In 2001, about 8 percent of the people in England were nonwhite. The largest minority group is made up of people from India, Pakistan, or Bangladesh. By 2010, Leicester is expected to become the first city in the United Kingdom—and possibly in Europe—to have a majority nonwhite population, primarily Indian. England is also home to large numbers of people from the Caribbean and China. In recent years, England has seen more immigrants from other parts of Europe. By EU agreement, any person from an EU country can move to any other EU country. Immigrants are now entering England from such countries as Poland, Hungary, and the Czech Republic.

England's Largest Cities (2001)

Greater London	7,172,091
Birmingham	977,087
Leeds	715,402
Sheffield	513,234
Liverpool	439,473
Manchester	392,819
Bristol	380,615

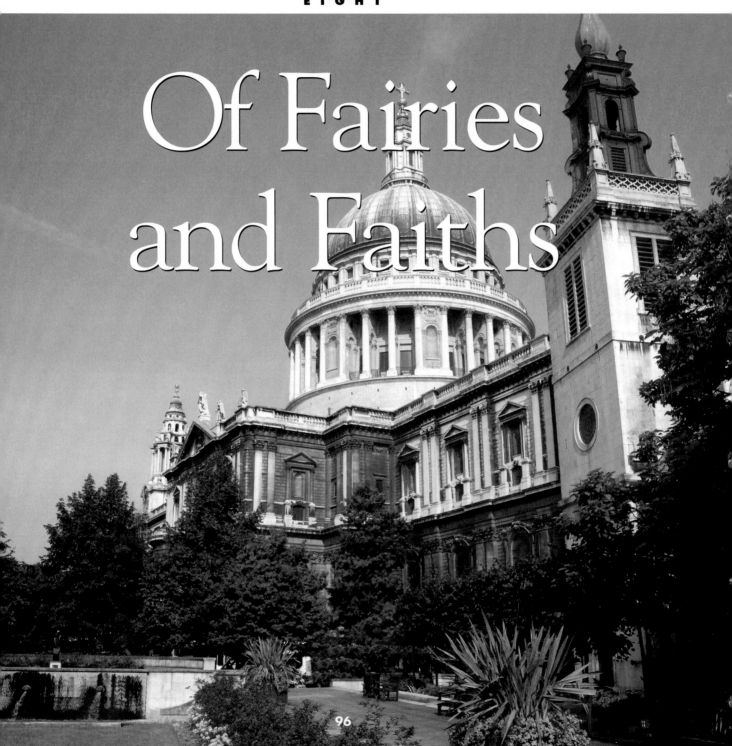

Of Fairies
and Faiths

M ANY NATIONS HAVE MYTHS THAT EXPLAIN THEIR early history or their creation as a people. The English were assembled from many different peoples who migrated to the island over the centuries—the Angles, Saxons, Jutes, and Vikings. The Celts were in England since before the Romans arrived two thousand years ago. The myths of today's English people thus originated in many different places.

English legends were filled with elves, fairies, hobgoblins, and sprites. William Shakespeare incorporated these

Opposite: **Important events such as royal weddings are often held in St. Paul's Cathedral.**

Ancient people erected these stones in Cornwall thousands of years ago. Experts today are not sure of their purpose.

Who Was King Arthur?

There was a real King Arthur. He was a Celtic leader who won twelve battles against the invading Saxons in about A.D. 500. From this bare-bones beginning, the legend of King Arthur grew. In the twelfth century, Geoffrey of Monmouth wrote about Arthur and his twenty-four Knights of the Round Table. Three centuries later, Sir Thomas Malory elaborated the story in *The Death of Arthur*.

According to legend, King Arthur and his queen, Guinevere, are buried at Glastonbury Abbey near Wells. Glastonbury was supposedly founded by Joseph of Arimathea, who is said to have brought the Holy Grail, a cup used by Jesus, to Glastonbury.

creatures—along with witches—into his plays. His fairies were usually tricksters who wreaked havoc on human affairs. England's main home-grown mythologies concern the legendary King Arthur. Robin Hood, who stole from the rich and gave to the poor, is another popular figure in English legend.

The Start of Christianity

Christianity took hold early in Ireland, Wales, and part of Scotland, but it was late coming to England. About A.D. 570, a Kentish king named Ethelbert married a Christian woman. In 597, Pope Gregory in Rome, hearing of the event, sent a mission to England led by a church leader named Augustine.

Augustine baptized the king and established Canterbury as the headquarters of the church in England.

It was the Roman Catholic Church that kept England from becoming an isolated island during the Middle Ages. Priests from the European continent went to England, and English priests studied abroad. They all spoke Latin, so when the Norman Conquest occurred, a number of people in England could communicate with the new leaders, most of whom spoke Latin as well as French.

Legend says that the Lilla Cross in Yorkshire marks the spot where a Christian saved King Edwin of Northumbria from being murdered. Edwin soon converted to Christianity.

Religious Beliefs in the United Kingdom (2001)

Christian	71.6%
Muslim	2.7%
Hindu	1.0%
Other	1.6%
None or none listed	23.1%

In 1533, Henry VIII married his second wife, Anne Boleyn. This resulted in the English church breaking from the Roman Catholic Church.

Reforming England's Church

For more than a thousand years, the Roman Catholic Church was the sole church in western Europe. Starting about 1500, some Christians began speaking out against the way the Catholic Church did things. Over time, these protesting groups broke with Rome and formed new Protestant churches. In England, Protestantism arose for a different reason: King Henry VIII wanted to divorce his wife, and the pope, the head of the Roman Catholic Church, would not let him.

When the pope refused to allow the divorce, Henry announced that the pope had no authority in England.

Parliament, acting at Henry's bidding, founded the Church of England and made the king its head. Henry had the Catholic monasteries, the large properties where monks devoted their lives to God, destroyed. He claimed their land and wealth. In small churches, people quickly removed Roman Catholic items, turning them into Protestant churches. For decades, families that remained Catholic had to keep their religious beliefs secret. Today, England is home to millions of Catholics.

The Official Church

The Church of England, or the Anglican Church, is the official church in the land. The monarch is its head. The church's two archbishops, one at Canterbury and one at York, are appointed by the queen. In 2005, John Sentamu, a native of Uganda, was named archbishop of York. It was the first time a black man had reached the top of the Anglican Church. The archbishops and the twenty-four bishops sit in the House of Lords.

About a million English people attend Anglican services every Sunday.

In 1992, the governing body of the church voted to allow women to be ordained as priests. Some male priests and church members were so opposed to this that they left the Church of England and joined the Roman Catholic Church.

The Salvation Army

An international semireligious organization called the Salvation Army was founded by William Booth in London in 1865. Booth wanted to bring God to poor people who were outside the established churches. Today, the Salvation Army is one of the world's largest charitable organizations. It helps the homeless in many cities, as well as people caught in natural disasters.

Other Churches

Protestant churches that are not Church of England are called Free Churches. The Methodist Church is the largest Free Church in England. It was founded by John Wesley while he was studying at Oxford University in the 1720s. He and his brother Charles started a group called the Holy Club. The members tried to grow spiritually through discipline, which they called "method." This gave rise to their name, Methodists.

The Baptist Church and the Congregational Church formed in England at about the same time, as did the Society of Friends, also called the Quakers. Founded by George Fox about 1650, the Quakers have no ministers at all. Instead, they believe that God speaks to each person individually.

Non-Christians

Jews first arrived in England during the Norman Conquest. Two hundred years later, however, Edward I expelled them. They began to return in the mid-1600s and gradually attained higher and higher positions in public life. London had a Jewish mayor in 1855. Three years later, Lionel de Rothschild was elected the first Jewish member of Parliament. Benjamin Disraeli became the first Jewish prime minister in 1868.

Few followers of Islam lived in England until the second half of the twentieth century. But in recent decades, a large number of immigrants have arrived from Pakistan, Bangladesh, and the Middle East. Britain is now home to almost two million Muslims. More than three hundred mosques—the Muslim houses of worship—are now scattered throughout the United Kingdom. The Central Mosque in London is one of the main Islamic institutions outside the Arab world.

Close to a million Indian immigrants live in England. Most of them are Hindus. They worship at many small temples and shrines. In 1995, the largest Hindu temple outside of India opened in North London.

Women place offerings on an altar at a Hindu temple in Watford. More than half a million Hindus live in England.

From Shakespeare to the Olympics

ENGLAND HAS MADE MANY ENDURING CONTRIBUTIONS to the world's culture. Nearly everyone has heard of the Beatles, Sherlock Holmes, Winnie-the-Pooh, Alice in Wonderland, James Bond, tennis, and Scrooge. The challenge for the English today is to live up to their past.

Opposite: **The English National Opera performs at the grand London Coliseum.**

Music Then and Now

Hundreds of years ago, wealthy families often employed a live-in minstrel—a musician who played and sang during meals in the great hall and for dancing afterward. Minstrels were especially popular at Christmas because people celebrated the entire Twelve Days of Christmas with gifts, good food, dancing, and plays until Twelfth Night on January 6.

Henry VIII composed simple songs called madrigals and accompanied himself on the lute. German composer George Frideric Handel lived most of his adult life in London. He wrote the great choral work called *Messiah* there. In more recent years, Edward Elgar wrote *Pomp and Circumstance*—often used at graduation ceremonies—for Edward VII's coronation in 1901.

The London Symphony Orchestra celebrated its one hundredth anniversary in 2004. Even before the orchestra started, one of the world's largest music festivals began. It is the series of Promenade Concerts, known as the "Proms," which are performed in London each year at the Royal Albert Hall. Many composers have created special music for the Proms, which

George Frideric Handel was a leading composer of religious music.

are broadcast on radio and television. An all-summer festival of opera is held at Glyndebourne in Sussex.

Starting in the 1960s with four boys from Liverpool who called themselves the Beatles, British pop musicians have conquered the world. Each decade, some of the biggest names in pop music came from England. In the sixties, it was the Beatles, in the seventies, Led Zeppelin, in the eighties, Boy George and Culture Club, in the nineties Spice Girls, and the 2000s are rocking to Coldplay.

Elton John, a native of Pinner in Middlesex, has long been a popular composer and performer. He won an Oscar for his songs for the Walt Disney film *The Lion King*. In 2005, his stage musical of the movie *Billy Elliott* opened. It tells the story of a young English boy who is laughed at for wanting to dance.

The Brit Awards are similar to the Grammy Awards in the United States. They've been given to both popular and classical musicians since 1977 by the British Phonographic Industry. In 2005, Devon-born teenager Joss Stone won several awards. Robbie Williams also won a special award for the best single from the past twenty-five years for his song "Angie."

A visitor studies paintings by Francis Bacon at the Tate Modern.

Artists

The aristocrats of England traveled abroad a great deal and often brought back wonderful paintings. An amazing collection of paintings has been gathered in the National Gallery in London. And the city's famed Tate Gallery doubled in size in 2000 when it opened Tate Modern in an old electric power station.

Many of England's greatest artists were portrait painters. Joshua Reynolds, for example, did beautiful pictures of children. Thomas Gainsborough is best known for his painting *The Blue Boy*. Because the English aristocrats loved their horses, one of the most popular painters was George Stubbs, who did memorable portraits of horses—and occasionally their owners.

John Constable made it acceptable for the artist to be interested in the countryside instead of aristocratic faces. J. M. W. Turner also painted landscapes, especially of the north. He was fascinated by what light and shadow did to scenes.

England's literary history dates back to *Beowulf*, which was written in about A.D. 700. Samuel Richardson, an eighteenth-century publisher, is considered one of the world's first novelists. His books *Pamela* and *Clarissa* were the first to tell long, connected stories that revealed the feelings and actions of the characters. His idea for a new form of literature enabled people to entertain themselves by reading instead of having to listen to a storyteller.

The First Best Sellers

Charles Dickens brought life to the English novel with *The Pickwick Papers* in 1836. This book concerns a group of young men from London who are determined to discover the English spirit. Like many of Dickens's books, it was published in sections in a newspaper. The story reflected current events and the voices of modern people. It was very popular. Readers waited avidly each month to learn what happened next. Dickens re-created his great success with such books as *Oliver Twist*, *A Christmas Carol*, and *Great Expectations*.

England soon produced many important female novelists, such as Jane Austen (*Pride and Prejudice*) and the Brontë sisters (*Wuthering Heights* and *Jane Eyre*). George Eliot (*Middlemarch*) kept her real name, Mary Ann Evans, a secret.

Many English writers have proven themselves masters of the mystery novel. Sir Arthur Conan Doyle created the world's most famous detective, Sherlock Holmes, who was blessed with incredible powers of logic. Writers such as Agatha Christie and Dorothy Sayers made the 1930s and 1940s the golden age of mystery novels. The adventurous spy James Bond, or 007, was created by Ian Fleming in 1953. John Le Carré turned spy novels into literary works in such books as *The Spy Who Came in from the Cold*.

H. G. Wells was one of the founders of science fiction. Born in 1866 in Kent, he used his science training to write *The Time Machine*, *The Invisible Man*, and *The War of the Worlds*. He also helped make some of the first movies.

The English have long loved fantasy, such as James M. Barrie's *Peter Pan* and Lewis Carroll's *Alice's Adventures in Wonderland*. In 1954, fantasy got a tremendous boost when J. R. R. Tolkien published the first two volumes of *Lord of the Rings*. Tolkien had been born in South Africa but moved to England as a child. He told his own children the story of *The Hobbit*, which was published in 1937. But it was many years before he created the entire Middle Earth world of his trilogy. In recent years, J. K. Rowling's Harry Potter books have dominated the fantasy market.

Agatha Christie's books have sold more than two billion copies in English.

Searching for Harry Potter

J. K. (Joanne Kathleen) Rowling was born in 1965. She studied French at Exeter University. Married and quickly divorced, she was left with a daughter to raise alone and no job. She used a space in her tiny apartment and a nearby pub in Edinburgh, Scotland, to write, something she had wanted to do since childhood. She created Harry Potter, Hogwarts School, and all the fantastic things that happen to him as he grows up and becomes a full-fledged wizard. The first book, *Harry Potter and the Philosopher's Stone* (*Sorcerer's Stone* in the United States), was published in 1997. When the sixth book hit the market in 2005, it achieved a world record for the most copies of a book printed at one time—10.8 million copies!

The Harry Potter movies were filmed in and around London. Harry Potter boards the Hogwarts Express

at King's Cross Station in London. But don't look for platform 9¾, where you might dive through a wall into a fantasy land. It doesn't exist. Hogwarts Hall of the School of Witchcraft and Wizardry, on the other hand, was filmed at Gloucester Cathedral. The fantastic library at Hogwarts is the Bodleian Library at Oxford University.

All the World's a Stage

Long ago, professional actors often wandered through the countryside, putting on plays wherever they could. In 1575, an actor names James Burbage stopped wandering and built a theater in London. Twenty years later, Burbage's followers tore down the theater, moved it to a new location in London, and renamed it the Globe Theatre. Plays by perhaps the greatest playwright of all time—William Shakespeare—were first performed at the Globe.

Shakespeare wrote comedies (*As You Like It, A Midsummer Night's Dream*), tragedies (*Hamlet, Romeo and Juliet*), and histories about English kings (*Henry V, Richard III*). For five hundred years, Shakespeare's plays have remained fresh. The Royal Shakespeare Company performs in London and in Stratford-on-Avon, Shakespeare's birthplace. Plays are also performed in the replica of the Globe in London.

London is still a center of world drama, with about a hundred theaters for live productions in use. One of these theaters has been showing Agatha Christie's play *The Mousetrap* since 1952. Andrew Lloyd Webber's musicals, such as *Cats* and *Phantom of the Opera*, are popular worldwide.

The new Globe Theatre was built exactly like the original theater in which Shakespeare's plays were performed. It has no roof, and many audience members must stand as they watch the action.

The Royal Shakespeare Company is one of the world's most famous theater groups.

A Sporting Chance

Many sports played today developed in England. These include soccer, tennis, rugby, badminton, and cricket. In private schools, young men were once expected to become hardy and develop good character and a sense of fair play by taking part in sports, even in lousy weather. Today, more people enjoy watching sports than playing them.

Hunting with hounds started in Saxon times, when wild cats and even wolves were hunted. Foxes became the target of organized hunting in the late seventeenth century. Foxhunters used fine horses to jump fences and large packs of dogs for the

According to legend, the game of rugby was invented at the Rugby School in Warwickshire in 1823. In fact, similar games had been played at Rugby and other schools for at least two hundred years.

Around the World

On November 28, 2004, Derbyshire-born sailor Ellen MacArthur set off from Falmouth on the south coast of Cornwall to sail alone around the world. Seventy-one days and fifteen hours later, an exhausted MacArthur returned to Falmouth, having broken the around-the-world record sailing time by more than one day and seven hours. The queen promptly made her a Dame of the British Empire. Dame Ellen plans to try to break other sailing records.

chase. Parties were held if the dogs caught and killed a fox. Gradually, though, the public began to view foxhunting as a cruel sport, and Parliament banned it in 2005.

English thoroughbreds are important racehorses worldwide. Queen Anne founded the Ascot Races in 1711. She wanted to have a course nearby when she stayed at Windsor Castle. Steeplechase was brought from Ireland to England in about 1790. In steeplechase, the horse must jump over hurdles. The Grand National is run at Aintree, a racecourse near Liverpool. The popular story *National Velvet* concerns a young girl and the horse she trains to run in the Grand National.

Given that Great Britain is an island, many English people enjoy spending time at the seaside. Surfing has become popular, especially around Newquay, in southwestern England.

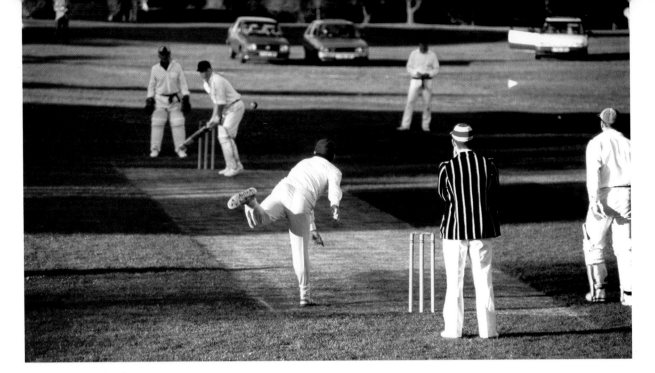

Cricket matches last anywhere from six hours to five days, depending on the form of the game being played.

The Cricket Wicket

Although cricket is played with a bat and ball, it bears little resemblance to baseball. Two sets of poles called wickets stand at opposite ends of a strip of ground called the pitch. A batsman tries to protect the wicket from a ball thrown by an opposing player. If the batsman hits the ball, he and another batsman at the other end of the pitch run back and forth between the two wickets as many times as they can. Cricket is at least seven hundred years old. Today, it is most popular in countries that were once English colonies.

The New Wembley

Soccer has been played in Wembley Stadium, called the "church of football," since 1923. In 2000, the English national team lost to Germany in the last game played at the original Wembley Stadium. The new Wembley Stadium opened in 2006. It holds ninety thousand people. Its most striking feature is an arch 436 feet (133 m) high, which is visible throughout most of the London area.

Football—The English Passion

Football, which Americans call soccer, is the most popular sport in England and the world. When Thomas Arnold was head of the private school called Rugby in the nineteenth century, he turned sports into a passion. He took the street game of football and gave it rules. In 1863, the Football Association was formed. Football was primarily an amateur sport until after World War II. Today, fans across the country proudly and loudly cheer on their favorite professional football teams.

The European Cup is awarded every four years to the best European football team. Liverpool won it in 2005. The World Cup is also held every four years, but it features teams from all around the globe. It has been held since 1930, but England has won it only once, in 1966.

Fans keep their eyes on the ball at a match between Chelsea and Liverpool in 2005.

Fans pack Trafalgar Square to celebrate England's victory in the 2003 Rugby World Cup.

The Rugby School, an elite school in Warwickshire, gave its name to another form of football in which an oval-shaped ball could be carried as well as kicked. Called Rugby Union Football, it is similar to American football, but the ball cannot be passed forward, and there are fifteen players to a team. In November 2003, England defeated Australia to win the Rugby World Cup. Three-quarters of a million fans welcomed the victorious team home to London. It was England's first Rugby World Cup victory.

The Olympic Games

The Olympics have been held in London twice, in 1908 and 1948. London will host the Olympics for the third time in 2012. Most events will take place in the Stratford section of East London. As the Olympic Stadium and other sites are being developed, Stratford City is being built to house the athletes. After the Games, it will be converted into a new community that will be home to five thousand families. Events will also be held in Greenwich, Hyde Park, and other spots in Greater London.

When the announcement that London had been selected was made on July 6, 2005, the British were very happy. The celebration ended abruptly the next day when terrorists bombs exploded on three London subway trains and a bus. More than fifty people were killed. The mayor began a "One London" campaign to pull together all residents, no matter what their national origin.

The Big Events

Tennis, a very old indoor game, moved outdoors to lawns in about 1870. The first lawn tennis championships were held at Wimbledon, outside London, in 1877. The world's most famous tennis matches are held there every year.

The Henley Royal Regatta is a four-day series of rowing races that have been held annually since 1839. The primary event is the Grand Challenge Cup, which brings eight-man crews from around the world to compete on the river Thames.

Another big event is the London Marathon, which is run each spring. Close to fifty thousand runners participate. It begins in Greenwich and ends in Green Park in Central London.

The Wimbledon tennis championships maintain many traditions. One tradition is that the players must wear white.

Life in England

FOOD FROM PRACTICALLY EVERY COUNTRY ON EARTH CAN BE found in restaurants around England. Immigrants from India, China, and other nations brought cuisines from their home countries. The English quickly learned to love these foods, with their different spices and textures.

Fast food is a tradition in England. Long before McDonald's and Burger King became widespread, the English bought quick meals at fish-and-chips shops. Fish and chips are french fries with deep-fried fish, usually cod.

Traditionally, the English upper class ate five meals a day: breakfast, tea or coffee at eleven, lunch, afternoon tea, and finally dinner late in the evening. Middle- and working-class people were likely to have fewer meals. For many people, afternoon tea gradually turned into a full supper, and the late formal dinner became a thing of the past.

Years ago, the English tended to eat large breakfasts of bacon or ham, eggs, breads, and perhaps a fish such as smoked herring. Today, "English breakfasts" tend to be found only in tourist hotels. Native English people typically eat smaller breakfasts.

Opposite: **England has a diverse population. About 8 percent of English people are nonwhite.**

Fish and chips are a favorite meal in England.

The English have always served wonderful meals featuring lamb. They also have found many ways to make mutton, which is the meat of older sheep, tasty and tender. Cornish pasties, which are small pies with chopped-up lamb, onion, and potato inside, are popular in many parts of the world. Yorkshire pudding is not a sweet dessert but a baked dough that tastes wonderful with good roast beef.

Houses

For much of English history, the houses of the wealthy were built with defense in mind rather than comfort. A wall surrounded the compound. The only way in was through a guarded gatehouse. Most activity of the family and its servants was carried out in one large room called the hall. Meanwhile, poor farmers lived in small cottages. The kinds of houses we know today were not built until around 1500.

Berry Pomeroy Castle, which dates from the twelfth century, has an imposing gatehouse and wall.

In recent years, the number of people in England who own their own homes has risen dramatically. In the twentieth century, town councils rented apartments or small houses cheaply to those who needed them. In the 1980s, the councils began allowing people to buy these houses. At the same time, many new houses were being built. In 1950, only 4.1 million homes were occupied by their owners. By 1996, that number had risen to 16 million.

At the beginning of the twenty-first century, however, property prices were rising quickly. They rose so much that many people who dreamed of owning a home are now unable to. This is especially true in London, one of the most expensive cities in the world.

Housing prices rose by as much as 20 percent a year in the early 2000s, making it difficult for many people to buy a home.

Winchester College is considered one of the best private schools in England.

Going to School

Education was a function of the church until the 1500s, when village schools began opening. In these villages, girls and boys went to school together. For generations, wealthy families sent their sons away to private school from the age of seven or eight. Probably the oldest private school is Winchester College, founded in 1382. Only about 7 percent of all children attend private schools today.

Girls of wealthy families were generally educated at home. They might later be sent to a finishing school on the European mainland, where the final "polish" was put on them before they "came out" (or made their debut by bowing before the monarch) and began looking for a husband.

Until the mid-1800s, the average working-class person might be able to read a bit but probably could not write. The 1870 Education Act made elementary education compulsory.

Children between the ages of five and ten had to attend school. By 1918, the age at which a child could leave school had risen to fourteen, and then to sixteen by 1972. Starting in 1944, a special test was given to all children at age eleven to decide who could eventually go to college. Over the years, many people objected to a child's future being decided at such an early age. During the 1970s, most schools were changed to mix students of all abilities.

At age eighteen, students take college entrance exams called A-levels. Today, about 44 percent of all students go on to universities or other higher education, a much higher percentage than in the 1960s and 1970s.

Walking Buses

School buses are rare in England. Instead, many schools use the "walking bus." Kids gather in groups with some adults and walk to school. Everyone in the "bus" wears a vest that reflects light because England has short days in the winter, and it may be dark when the students walk home.

Oxford University, which began in 1214, is the oldest university in Great Britain and one of the oldest in the world. Cambridge University was founded in 1284. Until the nineteenth century, these were the only universities in England. London University was started in 1828 for students who wanted to avoid the religion that Oxford and Cambridge emphasized. Since then, a number of colleges and universities have been founded.

The Open University is a higher-education system that grants degrees to students who don't go to a campus to live and study. They take their courses over television, by mail, or through a computer Internet hookup. Open University classes started in 1970. Anyone in the European Union can now take them.

Cambridge University is one of the top-ranked universities in England.

Communications

English people have been able to mail letters since the British Postal Service was founded in 1635. It was the first postal service in the world to issue postage stamps. The neighborhood mailbox—called a "pillar box"—was also invented in England.

More daily newspapers per person are sold in Britain than in any other country. The oldest weekly newspaper is probably Berrow's *Worcester Journal*, which began publishing in 1690. The *Times* of London began publishing daily in 1785.

Radio broadcasting began in England in 1922. The British Broadcasting Corporation, or BBC, started broadcasting television in 1936. It has no commercials. Commercial TV began in 1955. Since 1997, there have been three commercial services supported by advertising. The average English person watches more than twenty-five hours each week of broadcast TV and videos.

The *Sun*, which is famous for its celebrity news and sensationalistic stories, has more readers than any other English-language newspaper. It attracts five times more readers than such serious papers as the *Times*.

Looking Backward and Forward

London is home to the world-famous British Museum. It was founded in 1753 when Sir Hans Sloane, a doctor and naturalist who had traveled widely, died. He left the items he had collected to the nation. The huge building housing the British Museum opened to the public in 1847. Among the famous

The British Museum is one of the world's largest museums. It is home to more than one hundred thousand objects from ancient Greece and Rome.

items in the British Museum are the Elgin Marbles, massive statues from ancient Greece. The museum also houses the Rosetta Stone, which was carved more than two thousand years ago. Its discovery provided scholars with a way to translate ancient Egyptian writing. When the British Museum ran out of room, another museum, the Natural History Museum, was built to house just the natural history materials. Later, the Science Museum was added.

English Heritage is the government agency that decides which properties are important enough historically or architecturally to be protected. English Heritage itself is responsible for taking care of more than four hundred properties, including many castles. In addition, it has named thousands more properties that the owners must maintain. Every year in September, during Heritage Open Days, people can enter the Heritage properties free of charge.

The National Trust for Places of Historic Interest or Natural Beauty is a private organization that does similar work. More than two million members donate funds to buy and protect historic places. The National Trust also takes care of natural places. For example, it tries to buy sections of coastline that are in danger of being developed.

The Millennium Commission was established to develop and work toward plans that will improve British life in the twenty-first century. Financed by the National Lottery, it funds major projects throughout the land. The Millennium Commission has funded more than three thousand projects—from building bicycle paths and cleaning up environmental problems to rebuilding old city centers to supporting the arts. The face of England is being changed for the better, for a bright future.

English Holidays

New Year's Day	January 1
Good Friday	March or April
Easter Monday	March or April
May Day	First Monday in May
Spring Bank Holiday	Last Monday in May
August Bank Holiday	Last Monday in August
Christmas Day	December 25
Boxing Day	December 26

Thirteen towers rise along the outer edge of twelfth-century Framlingham Castle in Suffolk.

Timeline

English History

Celts begin arriving in England.	700 B.C.
England becomes a Roman province.	A.D. 43
The Romans build Hadrian's Wall across northern England.	ca. 122
Anglo-Saxon tribes begin coming to England.	ca. 410
The Anglo-Saxons convert to Christianity.	597
Norsemen (Vikings) take over English land.	840–897
Alfred the Great defeats the Danes.	897
The Normans, led by William the Conqueror, defeat the English at the Battle of Hastings.	1066
Thomas Becket is murdered in Canterbury Cathedral.	1170
The English conquest of Ireland begins.	1171
King John seals the Magna Carta.	1215
The Hundred Years' War is fought between England and France.	1337–1453
The Great Plague kills 1.5 million of England's 4 million people.	1349–50

World History

2500 B.C.	Egyptians build the Pyramids and the Sphinx in Giza.
563 B.C.	The Buddha is born in India.
A.D. 313	The Roman emperor Constantine recognizes Christianity.
610	The Prophet Muhammad begins preaching a new religion called Islam.
1054	The Eastern (Orthodox) and Western (Roman) Catholic Churches break apart.
1095	Pope Urban II proclaims the First Crusade.
1300s	The Renaissance begins in Italy.
1347	The Black Death sweeps through Europe.
1453	Ottoman Turks capture Constantinople, conquering the Byzantine Empire.
1492	Columbus arrives in North America.

	English History			World History	

English History	
Henry VIII breaks with the Roman Catholic Church and names himself head of the Church of England.	**1534**
The Spanish Armada is destroyed.	**1588**
The Great Fire of London destroys much of the city.	**1666**
England and Scotland unite.	**1707**
The Industrial Revolution begins in England.	**ca. 1750**
Britain loses its American colonies at the end of the American Revolution.	**1783**
The Duke of Wellington defeats Napoleon's forces.	**1815**
The Labour Party is created.	**1900**
The Irish Free State (now the Republic of Ireland) wins independence from the United Kingdom.	**1921**
India becomes independent of British rule.	**1947**
The National Health Service begins.	**1948**
Margaret Thatcher becomes Britain's first woman prime minister.	**1979**
Prime Minister Tony Blair takes Britain into the Iraq War.	**2003**
Terrorist attack London transport, killing more than fifty people.	**2004**

World History	
1500s	The Reformation leads to the birth of Protestantism.
1776	The Declaration of Independence is signed.
1789	The French Revolution begins.
1865	The American Civil War ends.
1914	World War I breaks out.
1917	The Bolshevik Revolution brings communism to Russia.
1929	Worldwide economic depression begins.
1939	World War II begins, following the German invasion of Poland.
1945	World War II ends.
1957	The Vietnam War starts.
1969	Humans land on the moon.
1975	The Vietnam War ends.
1979	Soviet Union invades Afghanistan.
1989	The Berlin Wall is torn down as communism crumbles in Eastern Europe.
1991	Soviet Union breaks into separate states.
1992	Bill Clinton is elected U.S. president.
2000	George W. Bush is elected U.S. president.
2001	Terrorists attack World Trade Center, New York, and the Pentagon, Washington, D.C.

Fast Facts

Official name: England refers only to part of the island of Great Britain. The official name of the country to which it belongs is the United Kingdom of Great Britain and Northern Ireland.

Capital: London

London

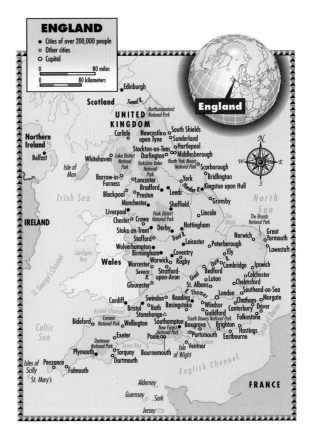

United Kingdom's flag

Wildflowers blooming

Official language:	English
Official religion:	Church of England
National anthem:	"God Save the Queen"
Government:	Constitutional monarchy
Head of state:	Monarch
Head of government:	Prime minister
Area:	50,352 square miles (130,410 sq km)
Bordering countries:	England is bordered by Scotland to the north and Wales to the west
Highest elevation:	Scafell Pike in the Lake District, 3,210 feet (978 m)
Lowest elevation:	Usually sea level, but when the tide is out near Ely in the Fen Country, a small section of exposed land is several feet below sea level.
Average annual rainfall:	East coast, 20 inches (50 cm) Western and northern hills, 40 inches (100 cm) Lake District, 130 inches (330 cm)
England's population (2004):	50,093,100 (United Kingdom: 59,834,300)

Population of largest cities:

Greater London	7,172,091
Birmingham	977,087
Leeds	715,402
Sheffield	513,234
Liverpool	439,473
Bristol	380,615

Stonehenge

Famous landmarks: ▶ *Windsor Castle*, Berkshire

▶ *The Tower of London*, London

▶ *Westminster Abbey*, London

▶ *Stonehenge*, near Salisbury

▶ *The city of Bath*

▶ *Canterbury Cathedral*, Canterbury

Industry: The most important mineral resource of the United Kingdom is oil, which is located in the North Sea. In England itself, however, coal has long been the most important mineral resource, helping to fuel England's Industrial Revolution. Sand, gravel, limestone, dolomite, and clay are also mined in England. England has one of the most industrialized economies in the world. Major manufacturing industries include iron and steel, electronics, and textile production. The United Kingdom as a whole is also one of the world's largest exporters of automobiles and has a thriving aerospace industry. English farms supply three-quarters of the nation's food needs. The chief crops are barley, wheat, potatoes, sugar beets, and rapeseed oil. England also has rich grazing land for cattle and sheep.

Currency: The primary unit of English money is the pound sterling, which is divided into 100 pence. In 2006, one pound (£) equaled 1.77 U.S. dollars.

Weights and measures: Metric system

Literacy: Virtually 100%

Currency

Kids from West London

J. K. Rowling

Famous English:

Jane Austen *Author*	(1775–1817)
Tony Blair *Prime minister*	(1953–)
Richard Branson *Businessman*	(1950–)
Winston Churchill *Prime minister*	(1874–1965)
Charles Darwin *Scientist*	(1809–1882)
Charles Dickens *Author*	(1812–1870)
Elizabeth II *Current monarch*	(1926–)
Henry VIII *King who broke away from the Roman Catholic Church*	(1491–1597)
Isaac Newton *Founder of modern physics*	(1642–1727)
Laurence Olivier *Actor*	(1907–1989)
J. K. Rowling *Author*	(1965–)
William Shakespeare *Playwright and poet*	(1564–1616)
Margaret Thatcher *Prime minister*	(1925–)
J. M. W. Turner *Painter*	(1775–1851)
Christopher Wren *Architect*	(1632–1723)

To Find Out More

Nonfiction

▶ Collins, Thomas M. *Tony Blair*.
Minneapolis: First Avenue
Editions, 2005.

▶ Deary, Terry. *The Barmy British
Empire*. New York: Scholastic, 2002.

▶ Morley, Jacqueline.
A Shakespearean Theater. New York:
Peter Bedrick, 2003.

▶ Myers, Walter Dean. *At Her
Majesty's Request: An African
Princess in Victorian England*.
New York: Scholastic, 1999.

▶ Nettleton, Pamela Hill. *William
Shakespeare: Playwright and Poet*.
Minneapolis: Compass Point, 2005.

▶ Oleksy, Walter G. *Princess Diana*.
San Diego: Lucent, 2000.

Fiction

▶ Cohen, Barbara. *Canterbury Tales*.
New York: HarperCollins, 1988.

▶ Garfield, Leon. *Shakespeare Stories*.
Boston: Houghton Mifflin, 1998.

▶ Green, Roger Lancelyn.
The Adventures of Robin Hood.
New York: Penguin, 1995.

▶ Lasky, Kathryn. *Elizabeth I: Red Rose
of the House of Tudor, England, 1544*.
New York: Scholastic, 1999.

Web Sites

▶ **Britannia**
www.britannia.com
*For all kinds of information about
British history, sites, and life*.

- **The British Monarchy**
  www.royal.gov.uk
  The official Web site of the British royal family.

- **The National Trust**
  www.nationaltrust.org.uk/
  For information about historic sites in England.

- **The National Virtual Museum**
  www.24hourmuseum.org.uk/
  To find out what's happening at many of England's museums and heritage sites.

- **Official Web Site for London**
  www.visitlondon.com
  The site includes interesting facts and figures about the city's history, culture, and economy.

- **Online BBC**
  www.bbc.co.uk
  This site is packed with information on history, sports, entertainment, and science.

Organizations and Embassies

- **British Embassy**
  3100 Massachusetts Avenue, NW
  Washington, DC 20008-3600
  (202) 462-1340

- **British Tourist Authority**
  551 Fifth Avenue, Suite 701
  New York, NY 10176
  (212) 986-2266
  www.visitbritain.com/

Index

Page numbers in *italics* indicate illustrations.

Meet the Author

Jean F. Blashfield delights in learning lots of fascinating things about places and the people who live in them. Sometimes she learns too much. When writing a book for young people, she's as challenged by what to leave out of the book as what to put in. This is especially true for the book on England because she's been there so often.

Blashfield first visited England on a college choir tour. Enchanted by what she saw, she made up her mind to go back. After developing the *Young People's Science Encyclopedia* for Children's Press, she kept that promise to herself and returned to London to live. She spent three years within the sound of the lions in Regent's Park, just around the corner from 221B Baker Street, where Sherlock Holmes is supposed to have lived. While in England, she visited the Lake District, Cornwall, and many places in between. She went to theaters, ballets, concerts, art galleries, and libraries, absorbing all she could of contemporary London. Since then, she has returned to England often.

Jean Blashfield has written more than 125 books, most of them for young people. Besides writing about interesting places, she also loves history and science. In fact, she becomes fascinated by just about every subject she investigates.

She has created an encyclopedia of aviation and space, written popular books on murderers and house plants, and had a lot of fun creating a book on women's exploits called *Hellraisers, Heroines, and Holy Women.*

Jean Blashfield was born in Madison, Wisconsin, and grew up in the Chicago area. She graduated from the University of Michigan and worked for publishers in Chicago and New York, and for NASA in Washington, D.C. She returned to Wisconsin when she married Wallace Black, a publisher, writer, and pilot, and began to raise a family. She has two grown children. Blashfield treasures her cats and her computers. In addition to researching via her computers, she produces whole books on the computer, scanning pictures, creating layouts, and even making the index. She is an avid Internet surfer, but she'll never give up her trips to the library, or to other countries.

Photo Credits